Perspectives on Communication in the People's Republic of China

Perspectives on Communication in the People's Republic of China

James A. Schnell

LEXINGTON BOOKS
Lanham • Boulder • New York • Oxford

LEXINGTON BOOKS

Published in the United States of America
by Lexington Books
4720 Boston Way, Lanham, Maryland 20706

12 Hid's Copse Road
Cumnor Hill, Oxford OX2 9JJ, England

British Library Cataloguing in Publication Information Available

Library of Congress Cataloging-in-Publication Data

Schnell, James A., 1955-
  Perspectives on communication in the People's Republic of China /
James A. Schnell
    p.   cm.
  Includes bibliographical references and index.
  ISBN 0-7391-0013-0 (alk. paper)
   1. Communication—Social aspects—China. 2. Communication—
Political aspects—China. 3. Communication in politics—China.
4. Communication in education—China. 5. Intercultural
communication—China. 6. Mass media—China. I. Title.
HN733.5.S36   1999
302.2—dc21   99-30451
                                                        CIP

Printed in the United States of America

⊖™ The paper used in this publication meets the minimum requirements of American
National Standard for Information Sciences—Permanence of Paper for Printed Library
Materials, ANSI/NISO Z39.48–1992.

This book is dedicated to my son,
Brian Lee Schnell

Contents

Introduction

China is as much a concept as it is a place. It has deep roots in the past (with a culture spanning 5,000 years) and is riding the wave of the present (with the founding of the People's Republic of China in 1949). China is commonly known as a very traditional society but the amount of change in China since 1979 has been far greater than what has been experienced in less traditional societies, such as the United States (during the same time period).

China has always been primarily an agricultural society. However, given the economic developments since the mid-1980's, parts of the Chinese population have advanced directly from functioning in an agricultural economy to an information age economy, bypassing the industrial and service economic stages. I have a friend in China to whom I remember explaining the concept of a "home telephone" in 1987. We now interact frequently via e-mail and he works in China's booming computer industry. He explains the newer communication technologies to me.

When visiting the major cities of China, one might incorrectly be lulled into a sense that China has shed its past and has adopted western values and lifestyles. This is a false assumption. China is wearing the cloak of modernity but the cloak covers the body of a traditional China. This traditional China, steeped in a feudalistic past, is neither better nor worse than the western world that exists in the U.S. But it is different. This book addresses many of the differences, with the intent of highlighting ultimate similarities.

The book addresses subjects in areas such as politics, education and health. Each chapter is written from my observations of a dynamic and constantly evolving China. These observations are based on my experiences in China and Chinese I have met.

I have been to China nine times. My first visit to China was as a professor at Northern Jiaotong University in Beijing (where I have returned as a guest lecturer since that initial teaching assignment). I am also a lieutenant colonel in the U.S. Air Force Reserve, where my assignment is as an assistant air attaché to China. Most important to me personally in this regard, though not directly related to the writing of this book, is being married to a woman from China. We were married in China, and I recognize our marriage as an example of the optimistic aforementioned similarities that exist between our countries. This book is dedicated to our child.

Section One

POLITICS

Chapter One

Bourgeois Liberalization:
The Labeling of Unwanted American Influences

In 1979, after being closed to the outside world for thirty years, the People's Republic of China reversed its policy of isolation by initiating a variety of economic, political, cultural, and educational reforms. The primary objective behind these reforms has been to modernize China and help it compete in the world market. Roughly one-fourth of the world population lives in China. The modernization of such a large country has involved a variety of obstacles.

One such obstacle has been how to import western technologies without importing western lifestyles. Increased interaction with the U.S. best exemplifies this situation. The People's Republic of China is a socialist society, governed by a communist party, and the U.S. is a capitalist society governed as a democracy. Thus, the Chinese government can benefit greatly from foreign interaction but stands to have its cultural values affected in major ways if this interaction is left unchecked.

The opening of China is a complex situation. China is comprised of a variety of cultures that date back thousands of years. An ironic contradiction to the Chinese way of life is the existence of Hong Kong in the south. Hong Kong, which was governed by England until 1997, is connected geographically but is miles apart ideologically. Hong Kong is very developed as a capitalist power in the world market. In 1997, China recovered jurisdiction of Hong Kong, and it will recover Macao (a similar type of capitalist area currently governed by Portugal) in 1999 and will be faced with the question of what to do with its control of two successful capitalist protectorates.

The current plan is for China to allow Hong Kong to keep its capitalist system for at least 50 years. This approach, referred to as "one country, two systems," will provide a testing ground for the acquisition of Macao and the intended acquisition of Taiwan. The recovering of Hong Kong is vaguely described by the Chinese government. "To keep Hong Kong's system unchanged, it is imperative to maintain socialism with Chinese characteristics under the leadership of the Communist Party" ("No Change...," p. 5).

The Chinese government has a sensitive task to deal with: how to praise (and adopt the developments practiced by) countries that have ideological perspectives which are contradictory to those of China. This presents an ideological tightrope, where the Chinese government must concurrently praise and condemn. It is obvious, even to the casual observer visiting China, that American values have found their way onto the Chinese landscape. American music, western clothing, and the widespread use of the English language attest to such developments in the popular culture. As the Chinese people embrace American technology they also seem to be embracing the American way of life. The Chinese government has labeled this negative practice as "bourgeois liberalization."

During my visits to China, I frequently heard this expression, or saw it in the press, but rarely could find a definition of it. Otherwise articulate individuals would become somewhat puzzled and confused when asked to define it. It was recognized as important but not easily defined.

The purpose of this chapter is to analyze the term "bourgeois liberalization" and describe how it is used by the Chinese government as a label for unwanted American influences. This discussion will be based on a review of literature written by and about the Chinese government and a written survey of student opinions at Northern Jiaotong University, Beijing, where I was a visiting professor. This subject is significant for speech communication scholars, as the term "bourgeois liberalization" exemplifies language which is created to be purposely vague. The term draws part of its meaning from this intentional vagueness. As discussed in this book, the term was created by the Chinese government to describe unwanted ideas and values which have been readily identified as American or western. When terms such as this are created, meanings are communicated through high context interaction processes.

In September 1986, the Chinese government issued a document entitled *Resolution of the Central Committee of the CPC on the Guiding Principles for Building a Socialist Society with an Advanced Culture and Ideology.* This official document defines bourgeois liberalization as "negating the socialist system in favor of capitalism" and goes on to say it "is in total contradiction of the people's interests and to the historical trend, and it is therefore firmly opposed by the masses" (*Resolution of the Central Committee*, p. 13).

The Chinese media consistently emphasize that the modernization of China must be done in accordance with the "four cardinal principles." The principles are "keeping to the socialist road, upholding the people's democratic dictatorship, upholding the leadership of the Communist party, and upholding Marxism-Leninism and Mao Zedong thought" (*Resolution of the Central Committee*, p. 4). The frequent emphasis on these principles by the

Chinese government can not be overemphasized.

China is eager to open to the outside world, but only on its own terms. The following paragraph provides a description of these terms.

> Closing one's country to external contact results only in stagnation and backwardness. We resolutely reject the capitalist ideological and social systems that defend oppression and exploitation, and we reject all the ugly and decadent aspects of capitalism. Nevertheless, we should do our utmost to learn from all countries .... Otherwise, we shall remain ignorant and be unable to modernize our own country. (*Resolution of the Central Committee*, p. 6)

This proposed objective is referred to as "socialism with Chinese characteristics."

China's embracing of American technology exemplifies a love-hate relationship with the American culture. Zhao Ziyang, former Premier of the State Council, underscores this situation in his *Report on the Work of the Government*. "Opening to the outside world is a basic policy of our state.... In 1987 we shall open wider to the outside world and explore new possibilities for the effective use of foreign funds, the import of advanced technology and the earning of foreign exchange through export" (Ziyang, p. 25). Deng Xiaoping, shortly before stepping down as the leader of China, stated a similar view. "The nation should emerge from its long-term seclusion and open itself to the outside world, because its development needs overseas capital, advanced technology and management expertise" ("Deng's Book Draws Lesson...," p. 4).

While praising interaction with the west on the one hand, Chinese leadership sharply warns of the dangers of adopting western values on the other hand. "We must not unthinkingly praise these western things, still less regard the decadent capitalist values and outlook on life as new ideas and disseminate them as such. Otherwise, they will contaminate and corrupt people's minds" (Ziyang, p. 34). Examples of negative western influences are frequently cited in the Chinese press. Some of these examples point to the corruption of youth, increased crime, the degeneration of literature, and misunderstandings in the universities.

Interaction with the west has been interpreted as both a problem and an opportunity for the youth of China. *China Daily* reported that "the motive for most crimes was money or sex oriented and that youth and juvenile delinquents were responsible for most of the cases" (Lixin, p. 1). The report continues, "Bourgeois lifestyles and publicity given to violence and crimes through films, television, pictorials and magazines stimulate teenagers to go astray" (Lixin, p. 1).

An interesting contrast in viewing western influences is provided in an article entitled "A New Way to Teach." This article describes how interaction with the west is changing the teaching of children.

> In the past we tried to mold children into ones who were not used to using their minds. But we cannot afford to do it to today's children, because they will enter a world full of competition. They have to be prepared to use their own questioning minds. (Xing, p. 5)

This unusual occurrence exemplifies an area where western approaches are preferred over traditional Chinese approaches. Generally, only western scientific technologies have been formally adopted.

Zhen Tianxiang, president of the Supreme People's Court, emphasizes the need to combat western influences to curb crime. He suggests "intensifying publicity about various laws and education in morality, ideals, discipline, and general knowledge, along with the efforts to resist all decadent and ugly aspects of capitalism" (Zhongshi, p. 1). Bourgeois liberalization has been blamed for literary problems such as rejecting the leadership of the Communist Party, divorcing art from politics and the encouragement of "sex literature." *China Daily* reports that "many talented young writers have been going astray and producing bad books due to the influence of bourgeois liberalization" ("In Literary Circles," p. 4).

A warning to writers was noted in April 1987. Zhang Xianliang, a leader of the National Committee of the Chinese People's Political Consultative Conference, stated that the "struggle against bourgeois liberalization will make Chinese writers politically more mature, better able to understand life and more perceptive to reality" ("Struggle Makes Writers...," p. 1). Six weeks later, in an article entitled "Guidelines For Literature," misguided writers were taken to task for their "incorrect ways." "Some writers, however, have forgotten their social responsibilities... spreading corrupt ideas, blindly worshipping foreign cultures and copying foreign things mechanically. This has been resented and criticized by the masses" (Danchen, p. 4).

Zhao Ziyang's *Report on the Work of the Government* stresses the necessary struggle against bourgeois liberalization. "If bourgeois liberalization were allowed to spread unchecked, it would adversely affect even more people (especially a part of the young people) who would lose their bearings, and it would plunge our country into turmoil..." (Ziyang p. 28). He concludes, "We must take a firm, clear-cut stand in relation to this struggle and never hesitate or waver" (Ziyang, p. 28).

The most widely publicized aspect of the campaign against bourgeois liberalization resulted after the pro-democratic student demonstrations that occurred in December 1986. Key leaders of the movement were criticized for their actions, and the protests were dismissed as misguided youthful exuberance. Yet the opening of China continues to pose problems on the campuses.

Robert L. Jacobsen, a writer for the *Chronicle of Higher Education*, wrote a series of reports on higher education in China. Regarding the opening of China, and its effects on campuses, Jacobsen quotes a group interview he conducted.

"Once you open your society," says one of China's more progressive university leaders, "you cannot close it again." But on hearing that, another official at the same institution retorts, "I've always believed that when you come to a turn in the road, you have to slow down." (Jacobsen, p. 42)

Chinese leaders do not underestimate the influence of student protesters, since many of them were once student protesters.

In April 1987 I surveyed the opinions of a class of graduate students I taught at Northern Jiaotong University in Beijing. The survey dealt with the development and meaning of bourgeois liberalization. All fourteen students in the class voluntarily participated in the survey. Their participation was not rewarded and the results were not shared. Their ages ranged from 24 to 26, the survey was done anonymously.

(SA — strongly agree, A — agree, N — neutral, D — disagree, SD — strongly disagree)

1. Bourgeois liberalization is reflective of western influences.

SA	A	N	D	SD
7%	36%	21%	36%	—

2. Bourgeois liberalization is more reflective of U.S. influences than any other country.

SA	A	N	D	SD
7%	21%	29%	29%	14%

3. Usage of bourgeois liberalization has become common within the last six months.

SA	A	N	D	SD
50%	43%	7%	—	—

4. Bourgeois liberalization ideals can be found in clothing.

SA	A	N	D	SD
—	7%	—	64%	29%

5. Bourgeois liberalization ideals can be found in dancing.

SA	A	N	D	SD
—	14%	7%	65%	14%

6. Bourgeois liberalization ideals can be found in music.

SA	A	N	D	SD
—	7%	7%	57%	29%

7. Bourgeois liberalization ideals can be found in literature.

SA	A	N	D	SD
—	72%	14%	7%	7%

8. Bourgeois liberalization ideals are becoming more common because of increased trade with the U.S.

SA	A	N	D	SD
—	57%	29%	14%	—

9. The best way to eradicate bourgeois liberalization ideals is to cease trade and interaction with the U.S.

SA	A	N	D	SD
—	7%	7%	36%	50%

10. If unchecked, bourgeois liberalization can become a serious problem in the People's Republic of China.

SA	A	N	D	SD
—	72%	14%	14%	—

11. Bourgeois liberalization means "negating the socialist system in favor of capitalism."

SA	A	N	D	SD
7%	43%	29%	14%	7%

The survey provided an uncommon opportunity to solicit student views on a sensitive subject. Opportunities to collect such data are far less common in China, compared to the U.S., due to the social and political climate. This consideration is discussed later in this chapter.

The survey indicates an increased usage of the term *bourgeois liberalization* in the six-month period prior to the survey, as 93% indicated that the term had not been common until recently (question 3). Bourgeois liberalization is far more evident in literature (question 7) than in other forms of expression such as clothing, dancing, and music (questions 4, 5, and 6).

Fifty-seven percent felt bourgeois liberalization ideals are becoming more common because of increased trade with the U.S. (29% were neutral) but only seven percent felt the best way to eradicate bourgeois liberalization is to cease trade/interaction with the U.S. (7% were neutral). These areas are covered in questions 8 and 9. Seventy-two percent agree (14% were neutral) that if left unchecked bourgeois liberalization can become a serious problem in the People's Republic of China (question 10).

Interpretation of the survey responses must be done in light of the fact that an American was collecting the information. Although their names were not connected with their responses, they did know I would be interpreting their responses. Aside from their possible reticence to share their thoughts with a foreigner they may have modified their views so they would not be offensive.

The media and students are readily aware of bourgeois liberalization and its possible effects in China but nobody seems to want any major crackdown similar to that experienced during the cultural revolution. The lessons of those years (1966-1976) seem to be too painfully recent to risk a similar situation. Perhaps this explains why only seven percent of students surveyed supported the ceasing of trade/interaction with the U.S. as a means of eradicating bourgeois liberalization.

The fears of any reaction against bourgeois liberalization which might resemble the cultural revolution period are evidenced in the press. *Newsweek* quotes a confidential party directive as saying "the party leadership urged communists not to allow their campaign against bourgeois liberalization— meaning western influences—to degenerate into personal vendettas against other party members" ("The Long Shadow of Mao," p. 40). Chinese leader Zhao Ziyang, in his *Report on the Work of the Government*, stated, "No attempt will be made to ferret out exponents of bourgeois liberalization at various levels, to implicate people at higher or lower levels or to have everybody make self-criticisms" (Ziyang, p. 30). He has emphasized that "no cultural revolution type political campaigns would be launched" ("On Student Unrest," p. 24).

A new phrase evolved in August 1987 which is an interesting follow-up to bourgeois liberalization. *Newsweek* reported "editorials that recently attacked bourgeois liberalization now denounce ossified thinking—a code phrase for positions that undercut Deng" (Deng Xiaoping's reforms) ("Deng's Balancing Act," p. 3). Ironically, the term *bourgeois liberalization* was coined to oppose reform, and "ossified thinking" was coined to promote reform. Governmental usage of such vague terms must surely be confusing for one who is trying to follow the party line. As indicated earlier, analysis of the term *bourgeois liberalization* is relevant to the speech communication scholar, as the term exemplifies language that is created to be purposely vague.

Devito (1986, p. 148) states that language is "a social institution designed, modified, and extended (some purists might even say distorted) to meet the everchanging needs of the culture or subculture." In this case, the term *bourgeois liberalization* was introduced, as there was a need to vaguely describe ideas and values which were to be discouraged but could not be accurately defined according to the communication context of the Chinese language.

The element of context is important in this understanding. "As we grow up in the world, our experience is formed by the language in which it is presented and talked about, and this language becomes so much a part of the mind as to seem a part of nature" (White, 1984, p. 276). Ochs emphasizes this degree of context more strongly in saying that "language is the major vehicle for accomplishing communication, language functions both *in* context and *as* context, simultaneously constructing and being constructed by the social occasion" (1979, p. 206).

Chinese people, and the Chinese language which reflects the culture, rarely communicate ideas in a direct manner. "Within Chinese conversational style is a tendency to respond in terms of expectations, goals, even models rather than mundane facts" (Murray, 1983, p. 13). The important role of context cannot be overstated when the aforementioned is paralleled with the system of government in China. "China's governance involves both the overt system of public institutions with whose members we interact rather easily and the more shadowy system of political and security organs whose work is not open..." (Murray, 1983, p. 10).

Thus, analysis of the term *bourgeois liberalization* indicates that the Chinese government communicates meaning on this subject in a manner which parallels the way meanings are communicated in day-to-day interactions in China. This process is defined as high-context communication.

Hall (1984) states that high-context cultures must provide a context and setting and let the point evolve. Low-context cultures are much more direct and to the point. Andersen (1987, p. 23) explains that "languages are some of the most explicit communication systems but the Chinese language is an implicit high context system." He goes on to explain that "explicit forms of communication such as verbal codes are more prevalent in low context cultures such as the United States and Northern Europe" (p. 24).

The term *bourgeois liberalization*, and to a lesser degree "ossified thinking," represent words which can be best understood in the high-context communication system which exists in China. The terms were created to be intentionally vague by the Chinese government to promote desired changes in China's political climate. While this system might be confusing to most

Americans (who are used to low-context interactions) this approach is more accepted in the Chinese culture (a high-context culture).

In conclusion, the opening of China provides a variety of opportunities for China to develop economically, technologically, educationally, and culturally. Similarly it offers western countries, such as the U.S., opportunities to expand in the same types of areas. Such development and expansion can be beneficial, but there is bound to be integration which creates conflict. Study of bourgeois liberalization provides an opportunity to better understand how one culture has chosen to deal with such a conflict.

References

Andersen, P. "Explaining Intercultural Differences in Nonverbal Communication." Paper presented at the 1987 meeting of the Speech Communication Association (Boston, Massachusetts).

Danchen, Chen. "Guidelines for Literature," *Beijing Review* (May 25, 1987), p. 4.

"Deng's Balancing Act," *Newsweek* (August 17, 1987), p. 3.

"Deng's Book Draws Lessons from History," *China Daily* (May 11, 1987), p. 4.

Devito, J.A. *The Interpersonal Communication Book.* New York: Harper and Row, 1986.

Hall, E.G. *The Dance of Life: The Other Dimension of Time.* Garden City, New York: Anchor Press, 1984.

"In Literary Circles," *China Daily* (April 17, 1987), p. 4.

Jacobsen, R.L. "Expectations Rise for Higher Education in China as Reform Temper Begins to Take Hold," *The Chronicle of Higher Education* (October 28, 1987), p. 42.

Lixin, Ma. "Meeting Over Youth Crimes," *China Daily* (April 21, 1987), p. 1.

Murray, D.P. "Face-to-Face: American and Chinese Interactions." In Kapp, R.A. (ed.), *Communicating with China.* Chicago: Intercultural Press, 1983, pp. 9-27.

"No Change in Hong Kong Policy," *Beijing Review* (April 27, 1987), p. 5.

Ochs, E. "Introduction: What Child Language Can Contribute to Pragmatics." In Ochs, E. and B. Schiefflen (eds.), *Developmental Pragmatics.* New York: Academic Press, 1979.

"On Student Unrest and the Question of Bourgeois Liberalization," *China Reconstructs* (May, 1987), pp. 24-27.

Resolution of the Central Committee of the CPC on the Guiding Principles for Building a Socialist Society with an Advanced Culture and Ideology. Foreign Language Press: Beijing, The People's Republic of China (September, 1986).

"Struggle Makes Writers More Realistic," *China Daily* (April 8, 1987), p. 1.

"The Long Shadow of Mao," *Newsweek* (March 16, 1987), p. 40.

White, J.B. *When Words Lose Their Meaning: Constitution and Reconstitutions of Language, Character, and Community*. Chicago: University of Chicago Press, 1984.

Xing, Li. "A New Way to Teach," *China Daily* (April 7, 1987), p. 5.

Zhongshi, Guo. "Chief Points to Obvious Drop in Violent Crimes," *China Daily* (April 7, 1987), p. 1.

Ziyang, Zhao. *Report on the Work of the Government* (Delivered at the Fifth Session of the Sixth National People's Congress on March 25, 1987), p. 25-30.

Chapter Two

Sovereignty and Reunification Controversy: China's Efforts to Influence Perceptions

In March 1996 *U.S. News & World Report* printed:

> A map of Taiwan suddenly filled the screen during the Chinese television news one evening last week. As a somber announcer began to read latitudinal and longitudinal coordinates of missile tests near Taiwan, a red box appeared on the map at the northeast tip of the island to mark one target zone. A second red box appeared southwest of the island. As the announcer read on, the boxes began flashing angrily. (Lawrence and Palmer, 1996, p. 53)

I, like millions of Chinese citizens, saw this report as I ate dinner in Beijing (the capital of China). I was in China during the period of the Chinese military exercises, held in the Taiwan Straits, and used this opportunity to gather data dealing with communicative efforts by the Chinese government to influence perceptions of in-country U.S. citizens, regarding U.S. credibility and intentions, related to the Taiwan sovereignty/reunification controversy. The exercises were staged to dampen the first-ever Taiwanese presidential elections on March 23, 1996.

The Chinese government uses three government owned and government controlled media channels to convey messages to English speaking foreigners (including U.S. citizens) who are in China. These channels are newspaper, television, and radio. China Central Television (C.C.T.V.) broadcasts English language news Monday through Friday at 9 a.m., 4 p.m. and 11 p.m. on channel 9. Each news report is about 15 minutes. China Radio International (C.R.I.) broadcasts English news periodically throughout the day on 91.5 F.M. Each news report lasts about ten minutes.

China Daily is an English language newspaper that is published six days a week (Monday through Saturday). It typically consists of about eight pages and is "China's national English language newspaper" ("China Daily," *China Daily*, 1996, p. 4). It began publication in June 1981. The main office is in Beijing, and there are seven regional offices throughout China.

Between February 21 and March 18, 1996, I listened to C.R.I. radio news each day, watched C.C.T.V. news each day it was broadcast, and read *China Daily* six days a week. I analyzed the broadcasts and newspaper reports for information that conveyed representative references to U.S. credibility and intentions regarding the Taiwan sovereignty/reunification controversy related to People's Liberation Army exercises in the Taiwan Straits. The most relevant period of reporting during this time frame was between March 6, when the military exercises were announced, and March 18.

Significant news information released by *China* Daily, C.R.I., and C.C.T.V. is controlled by the Xinhua News Agency. It is the central approving authority for news. Thus, significant news information conveyed on C.C.T.V. and C.R.I. is also reported in *China Daily*. Reporting in *China Daily* is more extensive than C.C.T.V. and C.R.I., because of its newspaper format, so I focused on collecting representative references from *China Daily*. Again, I did this with the knowledge that references made on C.C.T.V. and C.R.I. were also conveyed in *China Daily* (and the newspaper references were typically more lengthy).

Thirty-two articles were collected during the 27 days (February 21-March 18, 1996). This chapter will describe representative articles, in chronological order, that address U.S. credibility and intentions, with regard to the Taiwan issue. Since these stories were conveyed via English language channels it can be assumed that in-country U.S. citizens were targeted with this information.

On March 4, 1996, two days before the military exercises were announced, *China Daily* published an opinion article by Yan Xuetong, Deputy Director of the Centre for China's Foreign Policy Studies, entitled "China's Security Goals Do Not Pose a Threat to World, Analyst Says." In the article Yan explains, "If the U.S. stops its (arms) sales (to Taiwan), the peaceful reunification process (between China and Taiwan) will be accelerated. . . . China's nationalism has always been characterized by self-salvation instead of the egoistic tendency of western countries. . . . Only by preventing the arms sales by the U.S. to Taiwan can the peaceful reunification of that country be realized" (Yan, 1996, p. 4).

Also on March 4 a short article excerpted a story that had been published in *People's Daily* (the largest Chinese language newspaper published in China). The story briefly describes how U.S. diplomacy failed in creating support for its position against Cuba when the U.S. was criticizing Cuba for downing two U.S.-registered planes, owned by Cuban dissidents living in the U.S., that had invaded Cuban air space. However, "the U.S. failed to get the wide international support it had expected" ("Politics Behind . . .," *China Daily*, 1996, p. 4). This article is relevant because it provided context for the criticisms, lodged against the U.S. by China two days later, regarding U.S. diplomatic interference with Taiwan's move toward sovereignty, the implication being that U.S. diplomacy is consistently at fault.

On March 6 a front page article, featuring a map of Taiwan, announced missile tests to be conducted March 8-15 in the sea area near Taiwan. The article stated, "As long as . . . foreign powers, including the United States, stop arms sales to Taiwan, the tension will be relaxed" ("Missile Tests to Take Place . . .," *China Daily*, 1996, p. 1). The same day, a lengthy article, excerpting a report delivered by Premier Li Peng to the Fourth Session of the Eighth National People's Congress, stated, "Only when the principles enunciated in the three Sino-U.S. joint communiques are strictly observed and only when the two sides respect each other and refrain from interfering in each other's internal affairs will Sino-U.S. relations achieve sound development" ("Li Explains . . .," *China Daily*, 1996, p. 4.).

The military exercises near Taiwan began on March 8, and there were three articles that criticized U.S. foreign policy (an unusually high number of such articles) on the same day. One article protested a U.S. State Department report that was critical of human rights abuses in China. It stated that the U.S. should "do away with its wrongful practices of making unwarranted charges against other countries' human rights situations" and went on to label the missile tests as "a normal exercise designed to improve the military quality of the Chinese servicemen" (Xu, "China Protests U.S....," 1996, p. 1). Another article was also critical of the U.S. because facts had surfaced that "show a U.S. report on China's treatment of handicapped children to be a distortion" ("Official Refutes U.S. . . .," *China Daily*, 1996, p. 2).

A third article on that day, entitled "U.S. Still Uses Power Politics," describes how the U.S. has been at fault in its relations with Cuba. "The U.S. wants to cook up the incident to convert the attitudes of the international community. . . . The fruitless sanctions of the U.S. against Cuba also show the weaknesses and incompatibleness of the only superpower in the changing world" (Chen, 1996, p. 4). Parallels can be recognized between U.S. interference with Cuba and U.S. interference with the China-Taiwan issue.

The March 11 *China Daily* carried a short article and map that described how the Chinese military would be holding additional naval and air exercises in the Taiwan Straits between March 12 and March 20 ("Army Holds . . . .," *China Daily*, 1996, p. 1). A lengthy article (roughly 5500 words) was also included in the same issue entitled "Human Rights in China and U.S. Compared." The purpose of this article seems to be to criticize the U.S. for intervening in the internal affairs of another country, and it adds weight to its position by questioning the internal practices of the U.S. However, the legitimacy of some of the statements made would probably be suspect in the eyes of most U.S. citizens.

U.S. citizens.

The article begins, "American politicians have used the U.S. as a 'world human rights model' while wantonly attacking China's record on human Rights" ("Human Rights in China . . .," *China Daily*, 1996, p. 3). "Compared with the U.S., the constitutional rights of Chinese citizens are much more extensive and specific. . . . The Congress of the U.S. belongs to, is ruled by, and serves the interests of the rich. . . . Slavery did not die out completely. The Mississippi state legislature did not pass a law abolishing slavery until as late as February, 1995. . . . The top one percent of the population owns 40 percent of the country's wealth. . . . Half of the American people are illiterate. . . . One third of all U.S. women will be attacked by their partners. Moreover, 15-25 percent of pregnant women are beaten. . . ." ("Human Rights in China . . .," *China Daily*, 1996, p. 3).

The next day (March 12) three articles directly and indirectly address U.S. intervention in the Taiwan Straits. The boldest article assesses, "It was ridiculous that some people in the U.S. declared that the aircraft carrier Independence of the Seventh Fleet should sail towards Taiwan from its base in Japan, for intervention and even for defending Taiwan. . . . I think these people must have forgotten that Taiwan is a part of China's territory. It is not a protectorate of the U.S. . . . If they support Taiwan separatists' efforts, there will be a 'chaotic situation' . . . . An erroneous decision by the U.S. government in allowing Taiwan's Lee Teng-hui to visit the U.S. has since changed the once calm cross-Straits relations" (Ma, 1996, p. 1).

A related article adds, "It seems quite a few people from the west have a misunderstanding of the Chinese Army and that the mass media in the west have distorted the news about China in their reports" ("Western 'China Threat' Myth . . .," *China Daily*, 1996, p. 4). The third article concludes, "We mean what we say should foreign interference or 'Taiwan independence' appear some day: We will use all possible means to safeguard the unity of our country" ("Separatism Blamed for . . .," *China Daily*, 1996, p. 4).

Two articles appeared on March 13 that provide fairly concrete analysis of the situation. "The U.S. was warned yesterday by the Foreign Ministry to stop backing Taiwan's separatist activities. . . . It will be very dangerous if the Taiwan leaders interpret this signal as the U.S. Government's support and encouragement for its activities to split China. . . . (Referring to the U.S. Civil War) The U.S. also opposed outside interference, stressed national sovereignty and territorial integrity and was strongly against the sale of arms by a certain European country to the south" (Xu, "U.S. Told to...," 1996, p. 1).

A second article, also on the front page, establishes China's position. "There are two necessary conditions for peaceful settlement of the Taiwan question. . . . First, that Taiwan refrain from independence and separation; and second, that foreign governments not interfere in China's internal affairs and allow the Chinese people to settle the question on their own" ("'One China' Key to . . .," *China Daily*, 1996, p. 1).

The following day, further elaboration on the Chinese government position was provided. "Relations across the Taiwan Straits have always been haunted by the shadow of the U.S. . . . The U.S. may base its support for Taiwan on various excuses such as 'traditional obligations,' but the bottom line is that it is unwilling to see a powerful and unified China and wants to use Taiwan to contain China . . . . U.S. and Taiwanese politicians should not mis-interpret the justification and determination of the Chinese across the Taiwan Straits over reunification" (Guang, *China Daily*, 1996, p. 4).

On March 14, more speculation and opinion on U.S. motivations are described. "The world should be alerted to the fact a few powers are using human rights issues as a weapon against developing countries. . . . But some western governments are not happy to see a China that enjoys political stability and sticks to the socialist course. The U.S. and other western countries . . . turn a blind eye to their own problems while attacking China for its 'poor human rights record.' By doing so, they are trying to change China's political and social system which is the Chinese people's own choice" (Chen, "China Respects Human...," *China Daily*, 1996, p. 4).

Perhaps one of the most confusing articles, for the U.S. reader, appeared on March 15. The article opens and continues with "China urges the U.S. Government to 'take prompt and effective measures' to prevent the adoption of an anti-China bill in the House of Representatives. . . . We hereby express our firm opposition and strong indignation at it. . . . He blamed the U.S. naval fleet for causing set-backs to the stock market in Taiwan. When the U.S. conducts military exercises, no other country sends aircraft carriers to the region" (Xu, "U.S. Urged to...," 1996, p. 1). The article is confusing because it never describes what the anti-China bill is. The reader can only speculate it might have something to do with the U.S. sending Navy ships to the Taiwan Straits.

Two front page articles on March 16 briefly describe completion of missile tests in the Taiwan Straits ("Missile Tests Improve . . .," *China Daily*, 1996, p. 1) and new exercises to be conducted in the area between March 18 and March 25 ("New Military Exercises Announced," *China Daily*, 1996, p. 1). The articles made no mention of foreign interference. However, another front page article "accused the U.S. of adopting a double standard on wheat quarantine 'for its own interests.' It criticized the U.S. for what it described as a hegemonic act" ("Beijing Charges . . .," *China Daily*, 1996, p. 1).

A March 18 article resumed emphasis on China's position. "Any show of force by foreign powers in the Taiwan Straits will only deteriorate the situation.... Li (Premier Li Peng) declared that China would never accept the practice of others 'imposing one's will upon another'" ("Policy on Taiwan . . .," *China Daily*, 1996, p. 2).

On the same day a new topic was introduced regarding Chinese use of arms with the Taiwan situation. "A spokesman for the Chinese foreign ministry on Saturday refuted a report alleging that China has told the U.S. it will not resort to the use of arms in the Taiwan issue....China has never promised to abstain from resorting to arms....If something like 'Taiwan independence' or violation of Taiwanese space by a foreign force should occur, we certainly will use every means necessary to safeguard the sovereignty and territorial integrity of the motherland" ("U.S. Assertion Groundless," *China Daily*, 1996, p. 1).

Throughout the period that data were collected for this study, I watched for direct (low context) criticisms of U.S. actions in support of Taiwan and more indirect (high context) meanings that reflected unfavorably on U.S. foreign policy and the U.S. overall. This inquiry revealed that both kinds of messages were conveyed.

Low context messages, that are direct and explicitly stated, rely very little on the context provided in the situation whereas high context messages, that are indirect and implicitly stated, draw much of their meaning from the context or situation they are conveyed within. The high context meaning is portrayed more figuratively, much like a picture, and the low context message is spelled out with explicit wording in a literal sense. Consideration of low context and high context messaging is relevant because China tends to be more high context oriented and the U.S. tends to be more low context in the way meanings are conveyed. Thus, the Chinese media must consider the importance of broadcasting information using a low context approach so the American audience will correctly perceive messages as intended (as well as other English speaking receivers of such information).

The influence of the messages described in this article, regarding U.S. credibility and intention related to the Taiwan controversy, would vary depending primarily on the sophistication of the American news consumer. That is, the U.S. citizen that recognizes Chinese English language media as government controlled propaganda outlets can more realistically interpret messages as being propaganda rather than more objective news reporting. The U.S. citizen that interprets Chinese English language media the same way he or she would interpret U.S. media (that is, not recognizing that Chinese English language media is a propaganda vehicle) will be more inclined to be misguided in learning the facts of a situation. Similarly, a more sophisticated American television viewer will see a network news documentary as being more objective than a 30 minute paid political program sponsored by a political candidate.

Even when the U.S. citizen (in China) is aware of the aforementioned distinctions, he or she can be unduly influenced if he or she is only exposed to Chinese English language media and no (or little) information from non-Chinese sources. When I am in China I frequently listen to C.R.I. news, watch C.C.T.V. news, and read *China Daily* because I do not have easy access to non-Chinese media, and, even though I know it is government controlled propaganda, I consume the media with the intention of "reading between the lines" (inferring from what is reported) to speculate on what the facts of the situation are.

This approach is not always effective though. I was in China during the 1991 Persian Gulf War, and the Chinese government perspective of the war, as conveyed through Chinese media, was different than what was reported in the western "free press." Not until after leaving China did I learn the degree to which the U.S. had international support for its actions. Even when media is recognized as propaganda it still impacts the perception of the receiver.

Thus, Chinese media portrayal of U.S. credibility and intentions regarding the Taiwan issue likely affected the perception of in-country U.S. citizens, who consumed Chinese media and did not have easy access to western media. Again, the degree to which such Chinese media would be successful in conveying preferred meanings would primarily be based on the receiver's ability to consistently interpret the Chinese media as government propaganda, rather than as being produced by an independent free press.

References

"Army Holds Naval and Air Exercises," *China Daily* (March 11, 1996), p. 1.

"Beijing Charges 'Double Standard' on U.S. Grain," *China Daily* (March 16, 1996), p. 1.

Chen, Y. "China Respects Human Rights," *China Daily* (March 14, 1996), p. 4.

_____. "U.S Still Uses Power Politics," *China Daily* (March 8, 1996), p. 4.

"China Daily," *China Daily* (March 6, 1996), p. 4.

Guang, L. "Separatists Responsible for Cross-Straits Tension," *China Daily* (March 13, 1996), p. 4.

"Human Rights in China and U.S. Compared," *China Daily* (March 11, 1996), p. 3.

Lawrence, S.V. , and B. Palmer. "China Practices Pulling the Trigger," *U.S. News & World Report* (March 18, 1996), pp. 53-54.

"Li Explains Major Issues at NPC," *China Daily* (March 6, 1996), p. 4.

Ma, C. "China Resolved to Safeguard Sovereignty," *China Daily* (March 12, 1996), p. 1.

"Missile Tests Improve Troop Skills," *China Daily* (March 16, 1996), p. 1.

"Missile Tests to Take Place in Areas Near Taiwan," *China Daily* (March 6, 1996), p. 1.

"New Military Exercises Announced," China Daily (March 16, 1996), p. 1.

"Official Refutes U.S. Report on Child Abuse," *China Daily* (March 8, 1996), p. 4.

"'One China' Key to Straits Negotiation," *China Daily* (March 13, 1996), p. 1.

"Policy on Taiwan Never to Change, Premier Says," China Daily (March 18, 1996), p. 2.

"Politics Behind Worsening U.S.-Cuba Ties," *China Daily* (March 4, 1996), p. 4.

"Separatism Blamed for Taiwan's Recent Woes," *China Daily* (March 12, 1996), p. 4.

"U.S. Assertion Groundless," *China Daily* (March 18, 1996), p. 1.

"Western 'China Threat' Myth Groundless," *China Daily* (March 12, 1996), p. 4.

Xu, Y. "China Protests U.S. Report on Human Rights," *China Daily* (March 8, 1996), p. 1.

_____. "U.S. Told to End Its Support for Taiwanese Separatists," *China Daily* (March 13, 1996), p. 1.

_____. "U.S. Urged to Reject Anti-China Proposal," *China Daily* (March 15, 1996), p. 1.

Yan, X. "China's Security Goals Do Not Pose a Threat to World, Analyst Says," *China Daily* (March 4, 1996), p. 4.

Chapter Three

Using C-SPAN to Analyze U.S. Reaction to the Chinese Pro-democracy Movement

In recent years the academic community has recognized C-SPAN (Cable-Satellite Public Affairs Network) as a valuable teaching tool in the classroom. This chapter will describe how C-SPAN can be used for communications oriented research. Such application is exemplified by using my research entitled "Reaction in the U.S. to the Chinese Pro-democracy Movement." Discussion of this undertaking emphasizes methodology, thus enabling readers to realize possible applications in their own research areas. The primary method described stresses descriptive analysis of C-SPAN tapes obtained from the Public Affairs Video Archives at Purdue University.

Within my research area, cross-cultural issues related to U.S.-China relations, I have focused on reaction in the U.S. to the Chinese pro-democracy movement using C-SPAN as a representative forum for discussion on the issue. The types of programs analyzed are described later in this chapter. C-SPAN is a representative forum because it does not promote a political agenda. I will present this project in sequential steps.

1) I contacted the Public Affairs Video Archives at Purdue University and requested a selected listing of programs dealing with reforms in China. Tapes of all C-SPAN programs since 1987 are indexed at the Archives and are available from the organization, which prepared and sent me an annotated list of 82 programs (ranging in time from 30 minutes to ten hours and ranging in cost from $30 to $275).

2) Twenty-two programs were selected based on their relevance to the Chinese pro-democracy movement. Types of programs included forums, news conferences, speeches to the National Press Club, roundtables, House Committees, call-in shows, House Highlights, Congressional News Conferences, Senate Committees, and book reviews. These programs are listed in the suggested reading. The more relevant programs are noted in the discussion of classroom applications.

3) While viewing the tapes I prepared notes and, based on observed consistencies, decided to interpret the tapes through analysis of the high

context and low context messaging. That is, the high context channels of communication used by Chinese speakers conflicted with low context channels of communication used by Americans. Chinese speakers typically use high context channels of communication that tend to be indirect and heavily reliant on nonverbal messages. Meaning evolves from context. American speakers typically use low context channels of communication that tend to be direct and based on literal verbal statements. One can more easily understand the intended meaning without considering context.

This illustrates a standard cross-cultural communication dynamic. Cross-cultural misunderstanding can easily occur when interactants are using different channels on the high context and low context continuum. Analysis focused on statements by President George Bush, U.S. political representatives, Chinese students studying in the U.S., Chinese diplomatic representatives, and the American public. Analysis of these statements consistently reveals the Chinese preference for high context messages and the U.S. preference for low context messages.

The following situation exemplifies the importance of context when analyzing Chinese communication. During the period of June 1 through June 7, 1989 (the Tiananman Square shootings occurred on June 3), there was much confusion regarding who was in control of the Chinese government and what their position would be toward political and economic reform in China. There were rumors that Chinese leader Deng Xiaoping was dead and civil war was imminent. American politicians frequently made direct statements in support of the pro-democracy movement and called for the Chinese government to allow reform. The C-SPAN program "China Debate" (June 22, 1989) includes such low context messages. The Chinese government released no statements to clarify the situation.

However, when Chinese Premier Li Peng (a conservative hard-liner) appeared on Chinese national television wearing a "Chairman Mao uniform" instead of the more common western business suit, viewers could easily interpret the government's position. The context (what he was wearing) spoke far louder than what he was doing (performing ceremonial protocol). The "Chairman Mao uniform" was popular during the conservative reign of Chairman Mao Tse Tung. The fact Premier Li Peng appeared on Chinese national television wearing such clothing indicated he was in charge and that he was a conservative leader. Nothing needed to be stated. In a low context culture such as the United States, we would expect our leader to state his or her position rather than to have to interpret intentions based on clothing.

4) Findings from this analysis can benefit student understanding in a variety of courses in the communication arts curriculum including Mass Media,

Persuasion, Cross-Cultural Communication, Rhetorical Communication Theory, Interpersonal Communication, and Public Speaking. This can be done by stressing examples of pertinent course concepts evidenced in the C-SPAN tapes. In the Persuasion course, I emphasize the importance of diplomatic dialogue between nations, especially when the nations are in disagreement. The C-SPAN program "Bush Policy toward China" (December 12, 1989) describes National Security Advisor Brent Scowcroft's trip to China and President George Bush's policy of maintaining dialogue. This situation illuminates the relevance of diplomatic dialogue, and it exemplifies high context rapport.

In the Mass Media course, I emphasize the goal of objectivity stressed by news organizations. The C-SPAN program "China" (March 6, 1990) featured Mortimer Zuckerman (Editor-in-Chief of *U.S. News and World Report*) discussing his 1989 cover story "Inside China: The First Interviews with China's Leaders since Tiananman Square." His discussion clarifies the concern with objectivity, accuracy, and journalistic resourcefulness. It also exemplifies the role of U.S. media when they translate high context messages from Chinese leaders into low context meanings sought by the American audience.

In the Cross-Cultural Communication course, the influence of societal frames of reference is emphasized. China is a socialist nation and the U.S. is capitalist. The C-SPAN program "Sino-U.S. Relations" (March 9, 1988) features a speech by Chinese Foreign Minister Wu Xuequian. His speech describes China's reforming economy and its opening to the outside world. His subject exemplifies the difficulty of two systems, which have differing societal frames of reference, being able to find common ground. The high context messages of intention enhance this process. What applies at the international level frequently applies at the interpersonal level.

There are many who argue that scholarly research is done at the expense of time that can be put toward effective teaching. Use of C-SPAN in the aforementioned manner allows the faculty member to meet both objectives competently. Analysis of C-SPAN programming allows the faculty member to pursue significant scholarly research. As described in this chapter, such scholarly research has relevance in the classroom, and findings from this research are appropriate for scholarly publication.

References

"Bush Policy toward China." Call-In (December 12, 1989).
"China." Call-In (March 6, 1990).
"China Debate." House Highlight (June 22, 1989).
"Sino-U.S. Relations." National Press Club Speech (March 9, 1988).

Suggested Readings

"Almost a Revolution." Book Review (November 12, 1990).
"Anniversary of Tiananman Square Massacre." News Conference (June 4, 1990).
"A Worldwide Strategy for Freedom in China." Forum (August 4, 1989).
"Beijing Jeep." Book Review (January 29, 1990).
"CNN's Coverage of China." Speech (June 7, 1989).
"Future of Democracy Movement in China." News Conference (May 12, 1989).
"Human Rights in China." News Conference (June 4, 1990).
"Intolerance in the Name of Tolerance." Book Review (July 6, 1990).
"Legacies: A Chinese Mosaic." Book Review (May 27, 1990).
"Question Time." Forum (February 13, 1990).
"Recent Chinese Uprising." House Committee (June 15, 1989).
"Roundtable Discussion with Chinese Students." Roundtable (June 7, 1989).
"The End of the Line." Book Review (August 26, 1990).
"The Opening of China." Forum (November 19, 1987).
"Tiananman Diary: Thirteen Days in June." Book Review (September 20, 1989).
"Tiananman: One Year Later." Communication Today Presentation (May 16, 1990).
"U.S.-China Policy." Call-In (February 14, 1990).
"U.S.-China Trade." Call-In (June 18, 1991).

Chapter Four

The Lack of Political Cartoons
in the People's Republic of China

The influence of cartoons in society has been analyzed from various theoretical perspectives. Focus on the role of political cartoons is a specific area of study. This chapter deals with the lack of political cartoons in the People's Republic of China and how this void is filled through other means. Analysis will include description of the relevance of cartoons, the political situation in China, the lack of political cartoons, excerpts from Chinese media, and the promotion of a government subsidized hero (as a form of political cartoon).

Cartoons have long been recognized as a form of mass communication. "Since the comics affect the culture in a variety of popular expressions . . . they merit study as active forces in the development of national ethos" (White and Abel, 1963, p. 3). The influence of cartoons, or art-parables, has been emphasized by a variety of scholars.

"Art-parable can catch a strong man's conscience" (Short, 1968, p. 12). Denis de Rougemont stated, "Art-parable is a baited hook; a tender trap; a calculated trap for meditation" (Scott, 1964, p. 63). Picasso viewed art-parable as "a lie that makes us realize truth" (Hazelton, 1967, p. 16). "Art-parable then always has something to say; and for this reason it will always be more significant for mankind than mere entertainment ever could be" (Short, 1968, p. 15).

In a *Journal of Educational Psychology* article entitled "Comics as a Social Force," S.M. Greenberg wrote, "Comics as a social force came upon us silently and grew to considerable proportions before the guardians of culture were aroused by them" (Greenberg, 1944, p. 205). "The comics, in the first place, are potent communicators. . . . When Superman in 1940 zipped overseas and destroyed the Westwall, the Third Reich, in an abusive article in *Das Schwarz Korps*, branded the super-mundane comic hero a Jew" (White and Abel, 1963, p. 4).

The aforementioned example evidences how writers can use cartoons to convey desired meanings. Charles Schulz, author of "Peanuts," writes, "I preach in these cartoons, and I reserve the same rights to say what I want to say as the minister in the pulpit" (Schulz, 1965, p. 46). Thus, it is clear that cartoons can be used as political propaganda. In a politically oppressive society such as the People's Republic of China, I expected to find government use of political cartoons to persuade the masses and, to a lesser degree, less overt forms of political cartoons used by dissidents to oppose the government. However, political cartoons, as we know them in the west, are not common in China. An overview of Chinese society will provide needed context for understanding political communication in China.

Chinese civilization has a 5,000 year history that is grounded in feudalism. Feudalism emphasizes that personal expression, interests, and objectives are secondary to your position in society. Confucianism exemplifies feudalist thought. Confucianists argue that "the first step toward good government and the realization of a harmonious society was for each person to know his role and perform it well according to the strictest interpretation of that role" (Pye, 1984, p. 40). Feudalism was emphasized, especially since China's beginnings (roughly 3,000 B.C.), until 1911 A.D.

In 1911 the Nationalist Party overthrew the Ching Dynasty, the last dynasty in China. This began 38 years of turmoil during which China was forcibly opened politically and economically to the outside world. During this period the Communist Party was founded, the Japanese occupied China, and a civil war occurred between the Nationalists and Communists. The Communists, led by Mao Tse Tung, won the civil war in 1949, and they established the present political structure (the People's Republic of China).

China closed to the outside world from 1949 to 1979, primarily to reject foreign domination. Chairman Mao initiated a decade long cultural revolution in 1966 that led to massive persecution of Mao's real (and imagined) political enemies. Since 1979, China has engaged in a variety of reforms to help it compete economically with the west. These reforms have included very minor political reforms regarding rights of the individual.

The concept of feudalism has been constant throughout the history of China. One Chinese student told me, "It is who we are." Feudalism must be considered when analyzing Chinese society.

On June 3, 1989, the Chinese government ordered troops to stop a six week long mass protest on Tiananman Square (the 100 acre public plaza in Beijing). It is estimated that more than 3,000 people were killed. The student led protest was for an end of corruption in the Communist Party and greater rights for the individual. Since the massacre, the Chinese government began a massive crackdown on dissent, and a re-education campaign was undertaken. There was considerable opposition to the government, especially in the cities.

I reviewed Chinese print media (Chinese and English language) for examples of political cartoons but found nothing that strongly resembles political cartoons found in the west. The press is owned and controlled by the government, thus one can deduct that political cartoons are more a function of a free press (why would a government criticize itself?). One can find good-natured cartoons about Chinese life but these do not carry any type of political message. The government, as owner and operator of Chinese media, is far more interested in providing politically correct instruction for Chinese citizens than providing criticisms of the government. One example of politically correct instruction, conveyed through the visual communication mode, deals with the life of Lei Feng (a government subsidized hero). He will be discussed later in this chapter.

I have reviewed major Chinese print media (newspapers, magazines, and pamphlets), from three periods, in search of materials directly related to political commentary via visual communication. These three periods (1987, 1989, and 1991) represent different political climates in China. The year 1987 is seen as a good reform year, that is, political expression was freer in comparison to other years. Spring 1989 newspapers offer unique examples of political expression because this was during the massive pro-democracy movement that was supported by many segments of Chinese society (including journalists). The media in 1991 exemplify a return to strict government control, as the severe political crackdown was in full swing.

During March through June 1987, when I was a visiting professor at Northern Jiaotong University (Beijing), I subscribed to the English language newspaper *China Daily* and analyzed it for various types of cartoons. As previously indicated, 1987 is recognized as a good year regarding improvements with freedom of expression. Of course, this period ended abruptly in June 1989 with the Tiananman Square crackdown.

In 1987 artists and writers were encouraged to be socially responsible and politically correct with their art and literature. Wang Shen, Vice-Chairman of the Chinese Communist Party's Central Advisory Commission, stated, "If writers want to achieve anything, they must, first of all, have a correct stand and be dedicated to the people's cause" ("Mao's Talks...," 1987). Similarly, Zhang Xianliang, from the National Committee of the Chinese People's Political Consultative Conference, expressed that "literature and arts should serve the people and socialism" ("Struggle Makes Writers...," 1987).

A typical cartoon that was promoted by the Chinese government was an educational cartoon series, directed at children and adults, that included the following characters: Wise Grandfather, Little Tiger, Dear Sister, Well-Informed Boy, and Little Hedgehog. This series often dealt with social problems and the correct solutions to these problems ("Children's Paper Wins Trust...," 1987). I never saw a cartoon in this series that dealt with a significant political issue.

Warnings were found in Chinese media that gave writers and artists general guidelines to consider when dealing with political issues. The English language magazine *Beijing Review* carried such messages. "Some writers, however, have forgotten their social responsibility, producing bad and even vulgar works, spreading corrupt ideas, blindly worshipping foreign culture and copying foreign things mechanically. This has been resented and criticized by the masses" ("Guidelines for Literature...," 1987). The final sentence from the aforementioned quote is a high context threat regarding the government's resolute position to oppose such expression.

A 1987 editorial in the *South China Post* (a major newspaper in Hong Kong) provided a glimpse of what was to come two years later. "Students, who feel suffocated by an educational system that determines where and what they study and assigns jobs after graduation, are acquiring a taste for greater freedom. Officials are devoting much energy and editorial space to attacks on the very notion of individualism, calling it pernicious western import. They are demanding altruistic allegiance to a system that has lost almost all of its moral credibility" (Hood, 1987).

In mid-April 1989, students in Beijing began a protest movement that soon gained support from many segments of the Chinese population throughout the country. The movement was crushed six weeks later on June 3. Students staged a hunger strike on Tiananmen Square in May that fueled much of the support from non-student organizations (workers, farmers, professionals, retirees, etc.). Freedom of the press was strongest during this period. If liberal political cartoons were to exist this would be the time to find them.

The May 19, 1989, *China Daily* can be analyzed as an issue that represents journalistic reporting at the height of the movement. This issue is full of stories dealing with, and sympathetic toward, the protest. Five of seven cover page stories deal with the protest. The editorial page includes an article quoting Soviet leader Mikhail Gorbachev's support for political reform in China. The closest example of a political cartoon I have ever seen in a Chinese publication was below the editorial. It is a 6 x 10 inch photograph of a line of students holding hands and a small boy stretching between their legs to see what the excitement is all about. The photo's caption merely reads, "Revelations" (*China Daily*, May 19, 1989). The issue also includes a full page collage of eight photographs, with mildly sympathetic captions, from protest activities at Tiananmen Square.

Freedom of the press, or at least the Chinese version of it, left as quickly as it came after the June 3 crackdown. Indiscriminate shooting occurred throughout Beijing, intense persecution of dissidents began, and the media became a tool of the government to manipulate Chinese citizens. The crackdown continued.

The crackdown gained considerable momentum a year and a half after the June 3 massacre, when the world's spotlight was on the Gulf War. Thus, international scrutiny was less pronounced, allowing for greater political oppression by the government.

Review of Chinese print media during the U.S. ground war offensive into Iraq evidenced that the government clearly controlled the dissemination of information (government propaganda). The March 5, 1991, *People's Daily* exemplifies government emphasis on the aforementioned government subsidized hero Lei Feng. The *People's Daily* newspaper is published throughout China and has the largest circulation of any newspaper in that country. Four Lei Feng stories were featured on the cover page that particular day (*People's Daily*, March 5, 1991).

Lei Feng, who is now dead, is a "quasi-mythical model of the perfect communist man. . . . who spent his days overachieving and his nights reading Mao thought" (Willey, et al. 1987). He is frequently held up by the government as an example for Chinese citizens to follow. As previously mentioned, a random issue of *People's Daily* (March 5, 1991) carried four cover page stories about Lei Feng: 1) an editorial about Lei Feng as a model citizen and soldier, 2) names of selected Chinese citizens whose lives best exemplify the virtues of Lei Feng, 3) a conference held to study the virtues of Lei Feng, and 4) a travel agent who exemplifies Lei Feng virtues in her dedicated work with tourists. The visual omnipresence of Lei Feng is perpetuated through billboards, films, newspapers, books and pamphlets.

The lack of political cartoons in China is directly related to the lack of a free press in China. The closest it has to political cartoons are the "politically correct" cartoons dealing with Lei Feng. I expect if the government loosens its grip on the media, resulting in a less restrained media, more politically oriented cartoons will result with themes unpreferred by the government (as happened in 1989).

References

Berkman, A. "Sociology of the American Comic Strip," *American Spectator* (June, 1936).

"Children's Paper Wins Trust from Millions," *China Daily*, April 18, 1987, p. 5.

China Daily, May 19, 1989, p. 4.

Eble, K.E. "Our Serious Comics," in White, D.M., and Abel, R.H. *The Funnies*. New York, NY: The Free Press of Glencoe, 1963.

Greenberg, S.M. "Comics as a Social Force," *Journal of Educational Psychology*, Vol. 18 (December, 1944) pp. 204-213.

"Guidelines for Literature," *Beijing Review*, May 25, 1987, p. 4.

Hazelton, R. *A Theological Approach to Art*. Nashville, Abingdon Press, 1967.

Hood, Marlowe. "A New Spiritual Crisis Lights a Culture in Transition," *South China Post*, June 14, 1987, p. 13.

"Mao's Talks about Art Reaffirmed," *China Daily*, May 13, 1987, p. 3.

People's Daily, March 5, 1991, p. 1.

Pye, Lucian. *China: An Introduction*. Boston: Little, Brown Publishers, 1984.

Schulz, C. "Happiness is Lots of Assignments," *Writers Yearbook*, 1965 ed.

Scott, N.A. "Religion and the Mission of the Artist," in *The New Orpheus*. New York, NY: Sheed and Ward, 1964.

Short, R.L. *The Parables of Peanuts*. New York, NY: Harper and Row, 1968.

"Struggle Makes Writers More Realistic," *China Daily*, April 8, 1987, p. 1.

White, D.M., and Abel, R.H. *The Funnies*. New York, NY: The Free Press of Glencoe, 1963.

Willey, Fay; Elliott, Dorinda; and Carroll Bogert. "The Long Shadow of Mao," *Newsweek*, March 16, 1987, p. 40.

Chapter Five

High Context Messaging in
Chinese English-Language Mass Media

All communication can be placed on the low context-high context continuum. As stated in chapter one, low context messages are those messages that are directly stated and draw their meanings from literal statements. Receivers do not need situational context to accurately interpret the intended message meaning. An example of a low context message is, "Can I borrow $5? I forgot to bring money for lunch." The message is low context because the receiver has a low need to focus on the situational context. The message is clear. The speaker wants to borrow $5 for lunch.

A high context message draws much of its meaning from the situational context within which the message is conveyed. Consideration of literal statements is not enough for the receiver to accurately perceive the sender's message. A high context message, for the aforementioned message example, might be for the speaker to present the following meaning. "Silly me, I've gotten so forgetful lately. I even forgot to bring my lunch money today. I have too much on my mind today, I suppose. Lunch isn't really that important, though. The hunger pains will do me well as a constant reminder that I should not be so forgetful. This will be a meaningful lesson because I missed breakfast this morning as well."

This message, conveying that the speaker wants to borrow $5 for lunch, is presented in a high context manner. It is not explicitly stated. Rather, a general idea is presented (or, some might say, a picture is painted) that portrays the speaker as being hungry because he or she forgot to bring money for lunch. The high context listener can logically conclude that the problem can be averted with little difficulty by lending the speaker $5.

Each world culture fits on the low context-high context communication continuum. That is, each culture can be classified as low context, high context, or somewhere in between. Some of the more low context cultures include Switzerland, Germany and the U.S. Some of the more high context cultures include China, Japan and other Asian cultures. Thus, the U.S. citizen tends to present meanings in a direct literal manner and the Chinese person tends to present meanings in a less direct abstract manner. It is essential to remember that these low context-high context cultural perspectives are generalizations. They will not apply with all people in all situations in a given culture.

This low context-high context communication distinction exists on the interpersonal, group, organizational, and mass levels. That is, cultures that communicate high context messages on the interpersonal level will also communicate in a high context manner on the mass media level. This chapter describes high context messaging in Chinese English-language mass media. A case study analysis of said mass media, during the 1996 Taiwan sovereignty and reunification controversy related to People's Liberation Army exercises in the Taiwan Straits, is done as a means of focusing on one singular event. The exercises were staged to dampen the first-ever Taiwanese presidential elections on March 23, 1996.

Thirty two *China Daily* articles were collected during 27 days (February 21- March 18, 1996). This chapter will focus on representative articles from that collection, in chronological order, that exemplify the typical high context messaging found in the news reporting.

Two days before China announced the military exercises to be held in the Taiwan Straits, *China Daily* included an article about how "the U.S. failed to get the wide international support as it had expected" ("Politics Behind Worsening ...," *China Daily*, 1996). The article, excerpted from *People's Daily* (the largest Chinese language newspaper), describes how the U.S. tried to promote international condemnation of Cuba for shooting down two U.S. civilian planes that flew in Cuban airspace, but the U.S. efforts failed. This depiction of U.S. international relations weaknesses is relevant in that it set the stage for stronger criticisms the Chinese government would level at U.S. foreign policy within two days.

On the same day (again, two days before China announced the military exercises), an article titled "China's Security Goals Do Not Pose a Threat to World, Analyst Says," was included in the editorial page. The article creates a context for the coming military exercises announcement by explaining, "China is not and will never be a threat to either Western or Asian countries," "Drawing strength from the continued purchasing of advanced military equipment from the U.S., the separatists on the island (Taiwan) might pull further away from the motherland," and "If the U.S. stops its military sales to Taiwan, then it is certain that by 2010 the size of the Chinese military will be much smaller than the current level" (Yan, 1996, p. 4). A context is perpetuated that helps justify the coming military exercises.

On March 6, 1996, *China Daily* published a front page article titled "Missile Tests to Take Place in Sea Areas Near Taiwan," thus announcing the start of military exercises in the area around Taiwan. A map was included that showed the test areas. Shen Guofang, foreign ministry spokesperson, explained, "The tests will help improve the military competence of the People's Liberation Army" ("Missile Tests to. . .," *China Daily*, 1996). More important though, the exercises blockaded two of Taiwan's major seaports (Taibei and Gaoxiong), and this sent a high context message to Taiwan that it should cease separatist activities (seeking sovereignty from China) or risk Chinese military intervention.

The day after military exercises began, Swedish foreign minister Lena Hjelm-Wallen was quoted as saying, "Like other countries in the world, Sweden pursues a 'one-China' policy. That means we do not recognize Taiwan as an independent state and cannot have state-to-state relations with Taiwan" ("One China, Sweden Affirms," *China Daily*, 1996). This article, hardly newsworthy in and of itself, is a high context message that conveys the impression that the international community does not honor Taiwan sovereignty, Sweden included.

On the same day, an article titled "Military Is Purely for Defence Purposes" stated, "China's efforts to strengthen national defence and improve the quality of its army is purely for defence purposes" ("Military Is Purely . . .," *China Daily*, 1996). The article, published on the eve of the start of military exercises off Taiwan, does not mention Taiwan. However, it is clearly a high context message intended to create the image that the military exercises are related to a Chinese internal matter, thus implying that Taiwan is part of China.

The next day (March 8), in a story about China's rejection of a U.S. report detailing human rights abuses in China, the military movements were again described as "a normal exercise designed to improve the military quality of the Chinese servicemen" (Xu, 1996). Another article on the same day, about U.S. interference against Cuba, states that "the U.S. wants to cook up the incident (regarding U.S. licensed pilots who were shot down over Cuban waters by the Cuban military) to convert the attitudes of the international community that generally takes compassion on the island. . . ." (Chen, 1996). This is a high context message that indirectly draws parallels between U.S. interference against Cuba and U.S. interference against China, without mentioning China.

During the period of the military exercises, the U.S. and China were also engaged in a disagreement dealing with U.S. criticisms of human rights violations in China. A very lengthy article (roughly 550 words) appeared in the March 11 *China Daily* that compared human rights in China and the U.S. Some of the criticisms of the U.S. included: "Compared with the U.S., the constitutional rights of Chinese citizens are much more extensive....The Congress of the U.S. belongs to, is ruled by, and serves the interests of the rich....Slavery did not die out completely....The top one percent of the population owns 40 percent of the country's wealth....Half of the American people are illiterate. . . . 15-25 percent of pregnant women are beaten" ("Human Rights in China and U.S. Compared," *China Daily*, 1996). A high context effect of this overall message is that since the U.S. is wrong in its human rights record it is also probably wrong in its support of Taiwan.

On March 13, Chinese Foreign Ministry spokesperson Shen Guofang discussed the U.S. Civil War as a high context parallel with the tensions between China and Taiwan. "At that time, the U.S. also opposed outside interference, stressed national sovereignty and territorial integrity and was strongly against the sale of arms by a certain European country to the south" (Xu, 1996). The main message is that China, like the U.S. during the Civil War, opposes outside interference with its internal affairs.

In an article the following day, about the Taiwan controversy, a high context veiled threat was presented in the closing sentences of the article. "The reunification of the country is of vital importance to the Chinese people. To accomplish it, any cost might have to be justified" (Li, 1996).

The strangest of the high context messages appeared on March 15 in an article titled "U.S. Urged to Reject Anti-China Proposal." The article begins "China urges the U.S. Government to 'take prompt and effective measures' to prevent the adoption of an anti-China bill in the House of Representatives" (Xu, 1996), and it goes on to describe how the anti-China bill will harm U.S.-China relations. What makes this article particularly high context is that it never mentions what the anti-China bill is or what course of action the anti-China bill proposes. One could only speculate that the bill proposed U.S. military support to Taiwan if Taiwan was attacked by China.

On March 16 *China Daily* reported that the initial military exercise had ended and it was deemed a success. The exercise goals are indicated, none of which involve Taiwan independence, but a high context message is abstractly conveyed in a following sentence that deals with "reunification of the motherland." "The exercise achieved the desired goals in training the armed forces, improving the cadres' organizing and command abilities, testing the achievements made in scientific research and reforms of training, they said. The two commanding officers stressed that the SAF (Second Artillery Force) would resolutely implement the guidelines set in President Jiang Zemin's important speech, 'Continue to Promote the Reunification of the Motherland.'" ("Missile Tests Improve . . .," *China Daily*, 1996). Reunification of the motherland is generally thought to include bringing Taiwan, Hong Kong, and Macao under the control of the People's Republic of China government.

This chapter has described high context messaging in Chinese English-language mass media. The *China Daily* newspaper was chosen for analysis because its reporting is inclusive of the other two Chinese English-language mass media, C.R.I. (China Radio International) and C.C.T.V. (China Central Television). A case study analysis of this mass media, during the 1996 Taiwan sovereignty and reunification controversy related to the People's Liberation Army exercises in the Taiwan Straits, has been done as a means of focusing on one singular event. As mentioned, 32 *China Daily* articles were collected during 27 days (February 21-March 18, 1996) and analyzed.

Findings from this inquiry clearly evidence use of high context messaging in Chinese English-language mass media, using the *China Daily* newspaper as a representative mass media channel for analysis. The high context messaging found in Chinese English-language mass media parallels high context communication norms found throughout Chinese society.

References

Chen, Y. "U.S. Still Uses Power Politics," *China Daily* (March 8, 1996), p. 4.

"China Daily," *China Daily* (March 6, 1996), p. 4.

"Human Rights in China and U.S. Compared," *China Daily* (March 11, 1996), p. 3.

Lawrence, S., and B. Palmer. "China Practices Pulling the Trigger," *U.S. News & World Report* (March 18, 1996), pp. 53-54.

Li, G. "Separatists Responsible for Cross-Straits Tension," *China Daily* (March 14, 1996), p. 1.

"Military is Purely for Defence Purposes," *China Daily* (March 7, 1996), p. 2.

"Missile Tests Improve Troop Skills," *China Daily* (March 16, 1996), p. 1.

"Missile Tests to Take Place in Sea Areas Near Taiwan," *China Daily* (March 6, 1996), p. 1.

"One China, Sweden Affirms," *China Daily* (March 7, 1996), p. 1.

"Politics Behind Worsening U.S.-Cuba Ties," *China Daily* (March 4, 1996), p. 4.

Xu, Y. "China Protests U.S. Report on Human Rights," *China Daily* (March 8, 1996), p. 1.

_____. "U.S. Told to End Its Support for Taiwanese Separatists," *China Daily* (March 13, 1996), p. 1.

_____. "U.S. Urged to Reject Anti-China Proposal," *China Daily* (March 15, 1996), p. 1.

Yan, X. "China's Security Goals Do Not Pose a Threat to World, Analyst Says," *China Daily* (March 4, 1996), p. 4.

Chapter Six

East Meets West in News Reporting: A Comparison of *China Daily* and *China News Digest*

In March 1996 the Chinese People's Liberation Army engaged in military exercises in the Taiwan Straits in an effort to discourage Taiwanese independence initiatives. The exercises were staged to dampen the first-ever Taiwanese presidential elections on March 23. The situation was covered by the world press, and reporting about it provides an opportunity to study an English language newspaper (*China Daily*) in contrast with a western English language electronic newspaper (*China News Digest*).

China Daily is the government owned, government controlled English language newspaper distributed throughout China. It is published six days a week (Monday through Saturday). It typically consists of about eight pages and is "China's national English language newspaper" ("China Daily," *China Daily*, 1996). It began publication in June 1981. The main office is in Beijing, and there are seven regional offices throughout China.

China News Digest is a U.S. based English language electronic newspaper distributed to subscribers on the internet. It is published three to four times a week, and there are periods when additional special issues are published. It began publication in 1991.

Since *China Daily* is government owned and government controlled it is recognized as a propaganda vehicle for the Chinese government. Most of its important news is received from the Xinhua News Agency (the central approving authority for news in China). Thus, information conveyed in its pages reflect the thinking and perspective being promoted by the Chinese government. *China News Digest* is an independent electronic newspaper and draws much of its information from the western press and western news services. Thus, *China News Digest* is thought to present a more objective portrayal of events being reported.

This chapter will evaluate the timeliness and thoroughness of reporting about significant events related to the People's Liberation Army exercises in the Taiwan Straits. Timeliness refers to how soon reporting is done on the event, and thoroughness refers to the degree of depth addressed in the reporting.

Reporting by *China Daily* and *China News Digest*, on ten significant events related to the military exercises, is evaluated.

It is hypothesized that reporting in *China News Digest* will be more timely and thorough in comparison with the reporting in *China Daily*. The rationale for this hypothesis is that *China Daily* operates under more constraints, regarding what is reported and how it is covered, because it is government owned and government controlled. *China News Digest* is independent, so it has far fewer constraints. It draws most of its information from western news sources.

Reporting by *China Daily* and *China News Digest*, on ten significant events related to the military exercises in the Taiwan Straits, will be compared. The events will be described in chronological order, rather than in order of importance.

News of the aforementioned March 8-15 missile tests was reported in the March 6, 1996, *China Daily*. It was on the front page and included a map showing where the tests would be conducted. The foreign ministry spokesperson explained that "the missile tests are necessary to help safeguard the national sovereignty and territorial integrity of China" ("Missile Tests to. . .," *China Daily*, 1996). The spokesperson further explained, "As long as the Taiwan authorities cease their separatist activities, and foreign powers, including the U.S., stop arms sales to Taiwan, the tension will be relaxed" ("Missile Tests to . . .," *China Daily*, 1996).

China News Digest first reported news of the missile tests a month earlier on February 6 in an article titled "Mainland May Stage a Large-Scale Military Exercise Near Taiwan Soon" (Xu and Zheng, 1996). The article conveyed reaction from the Chinese Ministry of Defense, White House Press Secretary Michael McCurry, and U.S. Secretary of Defense William Perry. It also included a brief report of related activities in Taiwan. More extensive reporting was provided before the tests began on March 8. *China News Digest* was more timely and thorough in its reporting of the missile test announcement.

The second significant event (though not as relevant as other significant events) was indication that military growth in China will be affected, to a large degree, by U.S. sale of arms to Taiwan. The March 4 *China Daily* reported, "If the U.S. stops its military sales to Taiwan, then it is certain that by 2010 the size of the Chinese military will be much smaller than the current level" (Yan, 1996). The *China Daily* article was described the same day in *China News Digest* in an article titled "Beijing Can Cut Army if U.S. Halts Arm Sales to Taiwan" (Johnson and Xu, 1996). It quoted and paraphrased the *China Daily* article. Due to the nature of this event, being that the event was the *China Daily* article, *China Daily* and *China News Digest* are judged as equally timely and thorough in this case.

The third significant event was the meeting of Chinese Vice Foreign Minister Liu Huaqiu with Secretary of State Warren Christopher, Secretary of Defense William Perry and National Security Advisor Anthony Lake. The primary issue discussed was the Taiwan issue. *China News Digest* reported this event on March 6 (Zhang and Zheng, 1996). *China News Digest* was more timely and thorough in its reporting on this event in that *China Daily* did not report the event at all.

The fourth significant event was the actual firing of missiles, indicating the start of the military exercises. *China News Digest* provided extensive description of this event on March 8, including reaction in Asia, U.S. and Britain (Zheng, L., and D. Jia, 1996).

Reporting of the event did not occur in *China Daily* until March 12, and it was mentioned in less than a sentence. "The missile tests started last Friday while a naval and air exercise is to commence today" (Ma, 1996). On March 16 the Xinhua News Agency briefly reported, "The Second Artillery Force of the Chinese People's Liberation Army has successfully completed surface-to-surface guided missile launch training on the East and South China Seas between March 8 and March 15, with all four missiles hitting the designated target areas" ("Missile Tests Improve . . .," *China Daily*, 1996). *China News Digest* was more timely and thorough in its reporting of this event.

The fifth significant event was the expulsion of Taiwan and Hong Kong reporters from the war game area. Both newspapers reported the event on March 11 and did so in a similar manner (Zheng, "Five Taiwan and...,"1996 and "Army Holds Naval...," *China Daily*, 1996). The newspapers were equal in their timeliness and thoroughness of reporting.

The sixth significant event was the movement of the U.S. aircraft carrier *Independence* to the Taiwan Straits. *China News Digest* reported the *Independence* destination on March 11 (Zheng, "U.S. Air Carrier..." 1996), and *China Daily* reported the ship's movement on March 12 (Ma, 1996). Both reports were brief. The newspapers were equal in their timeliness and thoroughness.

The seventh significant event occurred when President Bill Clinton ordered a second aircraft carrier, the *Nimitz*, to move to the Taiwan Straits. *China News Digest* reported the event on March 12 (Zheng, 1996). *China Daily* did not report the event. Thus, *China News Digest* was more timely and thorough in its reporting of the event.

The eighth significant event occurred when the U.S. Senate and House of Representatives drafted a resolution encouraging the U.S. to be prepared to provide defensive weapons to Taiwan. This resolution was covered in *China News Digest* on March 12 (Zheng, 1996). The resolution was acknowledged in a

March 15 *China Daily* article that encouraged the U.S. to reject the "anti-China proposal" (Xu, 1996). However, strangely enough, the article never described what the resolution was. It merely referred to the proposal as being anti-China. *China News Digest* was more timely and thorough in its reporting on the resolution.

The ninth significant event existed when it was reported that the Chinese had told the U.S. that China would not take any military action against Taiwan. *China News Digest* reported the story March 15 (Zheng, 1996). *China Daily* reported the story March 18 but refuted the story as groundless ("U.S. Assertion Groundless," *China Daily*, 1996). The *China News Digest* was more timely in the reporting of the story but both newspapers were equally thorough.

The tenth significant event was a demonstration in Taiwan against China and for Taiwanese independence. *China News Digest* reported on March 16, "About 20,000 Taiwanese took their rage against mainland China's military intimidation to the streets. . . . Marching through the streets of Taipei, protesters chanted slogans such as "Taiwan Independence," "No Unification with China," and "I'd Rather Be a Taiwanese than a Chinese Slave" (Xu and Zheng, 1996). The demonstration was not reported in *China Daily*. Thus, *China News Digest* was more timely and thorough in its reporting of the event.

Reporting on ten significant events by *China Daily* and *China News Digest* has been evaluated with regard to timeliness and thoroughness of reporting. This evaluation concludes that *China News Digest* has been more timely and thorough in its reporting overall. It was more timely and thorough in six of the aforementioned ten significant events. It was more timely with one significant event but equal to *China Daily* in thoroughness with that event. *China News Digest* and *China Daily* were evaluated as equal in timeliness and thoroughness in the reporting of three significant events. *China Daily* was not evaluated as being more timely or thorough with any of the significant events.

The hypothesis of this study is accurate. Reporting in *China News Digest* was more timely and thorough in comparison with the reporting in *China Daily*. *China Daily* is government owned and controlled and therefore operates under more constraints to report information that portrays government views. Since *China News Digest* is independent, and draws most of its information from western news sources, it can be more objective in its reporting. I speculate that in similar comparisons between government owned and controlled media and independently owned media, independent media will be more timely and thorough, as *China News Digest* has been in this study.

References

"Army Holds Naval and Air Exercises," *China Daily* (March 11, 1996), p. 1.

"China Daily," *China Daily* (March 6, 1996), p. 4.

Johnson, A. and J. Xu. "Beijing Can Cut Army if U.S. Halts Arms Sales to Taiwan," *China News Digest* (March 4, 1996).

Lawrence, S.V. , and B. Palmer. "China Practices Pulling the Trigger," *U.S. News & World Report* (March 18, 1996), pp. 53-54.

Ma, C. "China Resolved to Safeguard Sovereignty," *China Daily* (March 12, 1996), p. 1.

"Missile Tests Improve Troop Skills," *China Daily* (March 16, 1996), p. 1.

"Missile Tests to Take Place in Sea Areas Near Taiwan," *China Daily* (March 6, 1996), p. 1.

"U.S. Assertion Groundless," *China Daily* (March 18, 1996), p. 1.

Xu, G. and L. Zheng. "Mainland May Stage a Large-Scale Military Exercise Near Taiwan Soon," *China News Digest* (February 6, 1996).

Xu, J., and L. Zheng. "Taiwanese Stage Demonstration for Independence," *China News Digest* (March 16, 1996).

Xu, Y. "U.S. Urged to Reject Anti-China Proposal," *China Daily* (March 15, 1996), p. 1.

Yan, X. "China's Security Goals Do Not Pose a Threat to World, Analyst Says," *China Daily* (March 4, 1996), p. 4.

Zhang, L., and D. Jia. "Three Missiles Fired, More Exercises Planned, Tension Increased," *China News Digest* (March 8, 1996).

Zhang, R. and L. Zheng. "Chinese Vice Foreign Minister to Meet High-Level U.S. Officials," *China News Digest* (March 6, 1996).

Zheng L. "Five Taiwan and Hong Kong Reporters Expelled from War Games Area," *China News Digest* (March 11, 1996).

_____. "U.S. Air Carrier Moves Closer to Taiwan," *China News Digest* (March 11, 1996).

_____. "News Summary: Latest Development of Tension in Taiwan Strait," *China News Digest* (March 12, 1996).

_____. "Beijing Says No Taiwan Attack," *China News Digest* (March 15, 1996).

Chapter Seven

Lei Feng: Government Subsidized Role Model

Context is important for the western reader when studying the People's Republic of China. The People's Republic of China is a politically repressive society. Political cartoons, as we know them in the west, are rare in China.

The following story exemplifies the importance of feudalism in relation to mass media. In the late 1770s, during the reign of the Qianlong Emperor, "a dictionary maker named Wang Xihou was found to have included in his dictionary the taboo temple names of the Qing emperors, so he was executed and 21 members of his family were enslaved. The provincial governor who supported the publication was also executed" (Fairbank, 1990, p. ix). Such an occurrence would send a clear message regarding the importance of following the wishes of government leaders. The message still exists today. "China's modern media have grown but operate today in the shadow of China's long heritage of central government autocracy" (Fairbank, 1990, p. x).

Chairman Mao Tse Tung's approach with opposing views parallels the feudalist theme evidenced in the aforementioned story from the Qing Dynasty. In 1956 Mao declared "Let one hundred flowers bloom and let one hundred schools of thought contend" (Lee, 1990, p. xix). Mao thus invited intellectuals to criticize the Communist Party. A year later, "having, in Mao's words, enticed the snakes (his critics and opponents) out of their holes, Mao launched an anti-rightist campaign in June, purging 550,000 intellectuals as anti-Party, anti-Socialist rightists, most of whom were sent to the countryside and deprived of their jobs and civil rights" (Lee, 1990, pp. xix-xx).

"The Chinese Communist Party is, more than any other Communist Party, both uniquely frightened of the people and yet wantonly scornful of them" (Binyan, 1990, p. 132). It is a peculiar situation. The government is both fearful and condescending regarding its view of Chinese citizens. What the Chinese leaders are doing "demonstrates that, as in the colloquial saying, 'They sit upon, and shit upon, the heads of the people'" (Binyan, 1990, p. 133).

On June 3, 1989, the Chinese government ordered troops to stop a six week long mass protest on Tiananman Square (the 100 acre public plaza in Beijing). It is estimated that more than 3,000 people were killed. The student led protest was for an end of corruption in the Communist Party and greater rights for the individual. Since the massacre, the Chinese government began a massive crackdown on dissent, and a re-education campaign is under way. There is considerable opposition to the government, especially in the cities.

I reviewed Chinese print media (Chinese and English language), from three recent periods, in search of materials directly related to political commentary via visual communication. These three periods (1987, 1989, and 1991) represent different political climates in China.

Analysis of Chinese print media focuses primarily on newspapers, magazines, pamphlets, and billboards. Print media examined does not include tatze-bao (wall posters) or other types of graffiti. I, as a native English speaker, received translation assistance with Chinese language materials from Chinese students and faculty colleagues. There was no selection criteria for materials to be reviewed. I collected materials wherever, and whenever, possible. Print media in China is not as abundant as in the U.S. I did not need to limit the scope of materials analyzed. Analysis of print media yielded so few examples of political cartoons that no classification scheme was developed (or needed).

I found nothing that strongly resembles political cartoons found in the west. The press is owned and controlled by the government, thus one can deduce that political cartoons are more a function of a free press (why would a government criticize its own members?). The government is far more interested in providing politically correct instruction for Chinese citizens than providing criticisms of the government. A prime example is the politically correct instruction stressed through the life of Lei Feng.

Lei Feng is a government subsidized hero. In *The Aeneid*, Virgil created Aeneas as the archetype for Romans to use as a role model. Aeneas possessed qualities that were admirable in the eyes of the Roman government (primarily to serve society). Similarly, Lei Feng is promoted by the Chinese government as a role model for Chinese citizens. Many quotes are attributed to Lei Feng, who died a worker's death (a telephone pole fell on him), that indicate the importance of serving Chinese society. "Such hero worship was common in the Maoist period, and many Chinese see it as another sign the hard-liners are trying to tug the country backward. By far the most famous cult is the one honoring Lei Feng . . . who has had a renaissance since the crackdown" (Kristof, 1990, p. C12).

"The Chinese Communist Party's superstitious belief in the power of the written word, in the power of propaganda, reaches astounding levels" (Binyan, 1990, p. 134). The western reader quickly sees considerable caution regarding political issues, in comparison to western-style journalism. "The Chinese Communist Party does not believe in the people because they cannot permit publication of any news item that might cause people to doubt the Party"

(Binyan, 1990, p. 134).

During my March-June 1987 visiting professorship in Beijing, I subscribed to the English language newspaper *China Daily* and had access to the Chinese language newspaper *People's Daily*. These are major national newspapers in China. I analyzed them for various types of cartoons.

Even a cursory review of Chinese publications will evidence the Communist Party's Four Cardinal Principles. These principles are 1) socialism, 2) the Communist Party leadership, 3) the people's democratic dictatorship, and 4) Marx-Lenin-Mao thought (*China Daily*, May 22, 1987). These principles are vague concepts that, in my mind and to native Chinese I interviewed, have no concrete meaning. Chinese interviewees, including Chinese students and faculty colleagues of mine, consistently indicated that these principles had little practical application. A parallel in the U.S. is the political rhetoric one hears during presidential campaigns (i.e., when a candidate claims to be representing the American people one is tempted to ask "Who are the American people?").

The State Media and Publication Office "has the power to stop publication of newspapers and periodicals. . . . Newspapers, periodicals, and publishing houses must have a clear-cut purpose in conformity with the Four Cardinal Principles and serving the building of a socialist society" (Lisheng, 1987). This type of vague guideline perpetuates a self-monitoring system whereby publishers, who do not have a definite ruling on what is appropriate or inappropriate, will most likely err conservatively rather than risk loss of their publication license.

"Things have been changed by the 1989 massacre. For the media, not only have 10 years of relative liberalization dissipated, but China's situation now approaches that of the Cultural Revolution (1966-1976)" (Binyan, 1990, p. 136). Thus, the press liberalization that occurred during the 1989 protests retrenched after the crackdown to a point far less liberal than had been permitted during the 1980s.

I was in Beijing during the U.S. ground war offensive into Iraq (February-March 1991). Review of Chinese print media during this period evidences that the government clearly controlled the dissemination of information (government propaganda). The March 5, 1991, *People's Daily* exemplifies government emphasis on the government subsidized hero Lei Feng. Four Lei Feng stories were featured on the cover page that particular day (*People's Daily*, March 5, 1991).

Lei Feng, who died in the early 1960s, is recognized as a "quasi-mythical model of the perfect communist man . . . who spent his days overachieving and his nights reading Mao thought" (Willey et al. 1987). Feng is frequently held up by the government as an example for Chinese citizens to follow. The four cover page stories about Lei Feng include 1) an editorial about Lei Feng as a model citizen and soldier, 2) names of selected Chinese citizens whose lives best exemplify the virtues of Lei Feng, 3) a conference held to study the virtues of Lei Feng, and 4) a travel agent who exemplifies Lei Feng virtues in her dedicated work with tourists.   The visual omnipresence of Lei Feng is perpetuated through bill boards, films, newspapers, books and pamphlets.

As I rode a bicycle around Beijing I saw a variety of Lei Feng billboards in front of different types of work units (i.e., factories, schools, government agencies, etc.). The billboards generally portray Lei Feng, in his working class clothes, looking toward the glorious future of China (as indicated in captions). A typical billboard caption states, "Long live the spirit of Lei Feng."   School children learn songs that praise Lei Feng. His diary is one of the more popular books.

A March 1990 *Beijing Review* article, entitled "Lei Feng Back in Limelight," describes Lei Feng in greater detail. *Beijing Review* is published by the Chinese government. "Millions of Chinese from all walks of life devoted their Sunday holiday on March 4 to serve others in various ways in a new nationwide upsurge to resurrect the spirit of Lei Feng. Lei Feng is quoted as saying, "A man has limited years, but to serve the people is an infinite cause.   I am resolved to plunge my limited years into the infinite cause of serving the people"("Lei Feng Back in Limelight," 1990).

The article goes on to report that Lei Feng is a popular topic among university students in Beijing and that he is an example to the Chinese people. "In learning from Lei Feng, we should do as he did—love the Communist Party and socialism, put our limited lives into the boundless cause of serving the people, work hard and practice thrift, and love and be devoted to our jobs" ("Lei Feng Back in Limelight," 1990).

A year later, the *China Daily* newspaper carried a similar story entitled "Beijing Learns from Lei Feng." The article reports that 270,000 Beijing young people served Chinese society by performing services such as watch repair, haircuts, and window cleaning ("Beijing Learns . . .," 1991). The *China Daily* cover page on the previous day features a photograph of workers giving free haircuts in an effort to emulate Lei Feng (*China Daily*, March 4, 1991).

A film called "Lei Feng: A Model Soldier" plays frequently on Chinese television. The film portrays Lei Feng's tireless dedication to Chinese society. The March 2 1991, *China Daily* television schedule indicates that the film played twice in one evening. It is worth noting that a film about Zhou Enlai only played once the same evening ("T.V. Programmes," 1991).   Regarding Zhou, *China Daily* reports, "In the history of China no man has been more loved and revered than the late Premier Zhou Enlai" (Bo, 1991, p. 5). For a Lei Feng movie to play twice on a night when a Zhou Enlai film only plays once can serve as an indication of Lei Feng's emphasis by the Chinese government.

It is interesting to find that, for as much as Lei Feng is promoted in China, little about him is distributed outside of China. I did a subject and author search on Lei Feng (in the U.S.) and found very few articles. These were fairly short overviews about his life. I wrote to *China Daily* to see about obtaining English translations of books and pamphlets about Lei Feng. *China Daily* indicated that material about Lei Feng has not been translated in English (Lee, 1991).

Regarding the pro-democracy movement in China, "there is a universal mood of resistance among students.... Real thoughts have to be hidden in order not to be punished" (Jacobsen, "Former Activists....," 1991). Lei Feng promotion is to be accepted as part of the political landscape. In 1991, a statement that criticized government propaganda was secretly distributed by former student activists in Beijing. "The propaganda material of the authorities contains alot of ultra-left points of view; even those with little common sense recognize this....A typical example is when the government orders writers to produce works glorifying Socialist China" ("The Movement Has Left a Job Unfinished...," 1991).

The closest things to political cartoons in China are the "politically correct" cartoons dealing with Lei Feng. I expect if the government loosens its grip on the media, resulting in a less restrained media, there will be far less emphasis on Lei Feng (as happened in the spring, 1989). The present day lack of political cartoons is directly related to the lack of a free press.

References

"Beijing Learns from Lei Feng," *China Daily*, March 1, 1991, p. 5.

Berkman, A. "Sociology of the American Comic Strip," *American Spectator* (June, 1936).

Binyan, L. "Press Freedom: Particles in the Air." In Lee, C.C. *Voices of China: The Interplay of Politics and Journalism*. New York: Guilford Press, 1990.

Bo, J. "Film Honours Zhou Enlai," *China Daily*, March 1, 1991, p. 5.

"Children's Paper Wins Trust from Millions," *China Daily*, April 18, 1987, p. 5.

China Daily, May 22, 1987, p. 4.

China Daily, May 19, 1989, p. 4.

China Daily, March 4, 1991, p. 1.

Eble, K.E. "Our Serious Comics." In White, D.M., and Abel, R.H. *The Funnies*. New York: The Free Press of Glencoe, 1963.

Fairbank, J.K. "Foreword," In Lee, C.C. *Voices of China: The Interplay of Politics and Journalism*. New York: Guilford Press, 1990.

Greenberg, S.M. "Comics as a Social Force," *Journal of Educational Psychology*, Vol. 18 (December 1944), pp. 204-213.

"Guidelines for Literature," *Beijing Review*, May 25, 1987, p. 4.
Hazelton, R. *A Theological Approach to Art*. Nashville: Abingdon Press, 1967.
Hood, M. "A New Spiritual Crisis Lights a Culture in Transition," *South China Post*, June 14, 1987, p. 13.
Jacobsen, R.L. "Former Activists from Universities in Beijing Report They are Reeling from Government Repression," *Chronicle of Higher Education*, May 1, 1991, p. A35.
Kristof, N.D. "China's Schoolboy Hero: Lesson is Lost on Many," *New York Times*, November 2, 1990, p. C12.
Lee, C.C. *Voices of China: The Interplay of Politics and Journalism*. New York: Guilford Press, 1990.
Lee, J.J. Professional correspondence from *China Daily* staff member (1991).
"Lei Feng Back in Limelight," *Beijing Review* (March 19-25, 1990), p. 9.
Lisheng, D. "China is to Improve Press and Publications," *China Daily*, May 16, 1987, p. 1.
"Mao's Talks about Art Reaffirmed," *China Daily*, May 13, 1987, p. 3.
Ming, R. "Press Freedom and Neoauthoritarianism: A Reflection of China's Democracy Movement." In Lee, C.C. *Voices of China: The Interplay of Politics and Journalism*. New York: Guilford Press, 1990.
People's Daily, March 5, 1991, p. 1.
Pye, L. *China: An Introduction*. Boston: Little, Brown Publishers, 1984.
Schulz, C. "Happiness Is Lots of Assignments," Writers Yearbook, 1965 ed.
Scott, N.A. "Religion and the Mission of the Artist." In *The New Orpheus* ed. New York: Sheed and Ward, 1964.
Short, R.L. *The Parables of Peanuts*. New York: Harper and Row, 1968.
"Struggle Makes Writers More Realistic," *China Daily*, April 8, 1987, p. 1.
"T.V. Programmes," *China Daily*, March 2, 1991, p. 6.
"The Movement Has Left a Job Unfinished," *Chronicle of Higher Education* (May 1, 1991), pp. A35-A37.
White, D.M., and Abel, R.H. *The Funnies*. New York: The Free Press of Glencoe, 1963.
Willey, F.; Elliott, D.; and Bogert, C. "The Long Shadow of Mao," *Newsweek*, March 16, 1987, p. 40.

Section Two

EDUCATION

Chapter Eight

Academic Departments in China

This chapter will describe the management of university academic departments in The People's Republic of China. I used the opportunity of being a visiting professor at Northern Jiaotong University, Beijing, to study how academic departments are managed and how faculty are motivated through reward systems. Such inquiry is relevant as there are many parallels between the functioning of academic departments in the U.S. and China. Comparison and contrast can provide enhanced understanding of both approaches.

Academic departments in China have parallels with academic departments in the United States, but there are marked differences. The management of academic departments in China is based on the unique development of that country.

In 1949, the People's Republic of China was established and for the next 30 years China was essentially a closed society to the outside world. There was limited interaction with other countries and thus little knowledge of how foreign academic departments were managed. The only exception to this is the Soviet academic system, as China did maintain ties with the Soviet Union during this period.

Between 1966 and 1976, China experienced a "cultural revolution." During this time education was criticized and changed drastically. Universities were shut down for the most part. Many administrators and intellectuals were taken from their positions and forced to work in the countryside in "re-education camps." All books were banned except for works by and about Chairman Mao Tse Tung (the Chinese leader at the time). Students were taught primarily about the basics of agriculture (i.e., planting and harvesting of crops). This period, which ended with the death of Chairman Mao, stunned the growth of education in China.

In 1979, an open door policy was implemented in an effort to help China compete with the outside world. Since that time, trade and joint business ventures with the west have been emphasized strongly, specifically with the United States. As interaction with the west increases, Chinese academic departments have worked to learn from practices of academic departments in the west. Each year, educational exchanges involving students, faculty, and administrators occur between China and the United States. The learning process is a two way street.

Higher education in China has shifted from academic approaches practiced in the former Soviet Union and has begun to adopt practices used in the U.S. Thus, the Chinese are "trying to make their universities more comprehensive institutions in which teaching and research are expected to reinforce one another" (Jacobsen, October 28, 1987, p. 41). The Soviet approach puts far more emphasis on research.

Northern Jiaotong University, in Beijing, exemplifies a typical university in China, and the administration of its academic departments is consistent with government regulations. A brief description of the university structure, and the role of the academic chairpersons within this structure, will clarify some of the similarities and differences with university structures in the United States.

Faculty members generally teach two semesters (17 weeks each) a year and teach roughly eight hours a week. Aside from teaching, some faculty members will research teaching methods and subject areas which are pertinent to their expertise. Annual salaries vary between 1,000 to 1,800 yuan ($300 to $500) a year and annual bonuses equal about 25% of their salary. Salaries are the same at each level (instructor, assistant professor, associate professor, and full professor), but bonuses vary within each level. Thus, the bonus system is similar to the merit pay system in the U.S.

Nonmarried faculty members live four to a room (about the size of a typical U.S. dormitory room) and they can be given their own room after about 5 to 6 years. Rent is minimal (proportionate to an American paying $5 U.S. a month). A retirement pension is provided by the government. Housing is based on position, age, marital status, and membership in the Communist Party.

Key differences between the Chinese and U.S. systems deal with professors serving as role models and the selection of who will work as professors. Teachers in China are expected to serve as role models in moral as well as academic and development areas. Li Xingwan, vice-chairman of the Chinese Educational Workers' Union (CEWU), emphasizes the importance of moral development. He states, "CEWU and its branches should encourage teachers to improve themselves and turn the younger generation into one devoted to socialism with high moral standards, academic knowledge and discipline" (Li Xing, 1987, p. 3).

Academic faculties stereotypically are overworked and underpaid, and living conditions are inferior. Thus, the teaching profession is not as popular as it is in the U.S. For example, Yang Chuanwei, President of the Beijing Teachers College, reports that the number of people who want to join academic faculties has dropped considerably. "Out of 802 students enrolled by the college last year, there were only 57 who had selected the college as their first choice for higher education" (Yang Chuanwei, 1987, p. 4).

I conducted a written survey of students who were enrolled in the teachers training program at Northern Jiaotong University. Two questions from the survey solicited their opinions regarding teachers serving as role models and placement of the students in the teacher training program.

Twenty students were asked to respond to the following statements: 1) "As an English teacher, my behavior will serve as an important role model for my students regarding social responsibility," and 2) "Teaching english was my first choice over other types of jobs." They were asked to strongly agree (SA), agree (A), neutral (N), disagree (D) and strongly disagree (SD).

The following table indicates students' responses.

Question 1	SA	A	N	D	SD
(moral role model)	35%	45%	15%	5%	—
Question 2	SA	A	N	D	SD
(selected teaching)	10%	20%	—	35%	35%

Thus, the environment within which Chinese and U.S. academic chairpersons work, differs.

Academic chairpersons are appointed by the university president. No evaluation is done by superiors or subordinates. Primary criteria for selection is based on position (associate or full professor) and productivity in research. A faculty member must have at least a B.A. degree before being promoted to associate professor. The following graph provides a description of the university chain of command.

University President

Teaching Staff Director
Department Head

Vice-Head (Research) ————————————————— Vice-Head (Teaching)

F - A - C - U - L - T - Y

The Department of Language Study at Northern Jiaotong University exemplifies a typical department within the university. There are forty faculty members who teach graduate and undergraduate courses. Primary courses of instruction deal with English as a major area of study and English as a second language (a minor area of study). The department has 150 English majors and 1200 students studying English as a second language.

The morale and motivation of faculty, and the role of the academic chairperson in these processes, are unique situations compared to the United

States. Tenure and academic freedom, as we know it in the U.S., does not exist in China. Faculty members "belong" to their universities for life. They cannot change occupations or move to another university without strong connections in the central government. They also cannot be fired by the academic chairperson. Faculty appointments are in effect until mandatory retirement (55 for women and 60 for men). When I shared my pleasure with receiving tenure in the U.S., my Chinese counterparts did not see this as especially good or bad news since their teaching assignments are permanent. When I moved to another unrelated academic institution, they perceived this as very unusual. With such a system, many Chinese universities have a very low student-faculty ratio. At Beijing University the ratio is about 4 to 1. Lao Ze Yi, President of West China University of Medical Sciences, states, "If they do a good job or don't do a good job, they still keep their positions.... We can't fire anybody" (Jacobsen, October 28, 1987, p. 42).

Faculty members can move around within a department, though. For instance, they can teach undergraduate or graduate students and required or elective courses, and they can focus more on teaching or research (depending upon the needs of the department). Academic chairpersons have direct control over such moves.

Motivation of faculty is seen as a primary problem. Often the more seniority a faculty member has the less likely he or she will be productive beyond teaching his or her assigned classes. Academic chairpersons can refer those who need motivation to the university "Head of Propaganda" and encourage them to attend weekly political meetings so they might learn more about the "socialist struggle."

In more serious cases, an unproductive faculty member will go through a series of warnings. First, the unproductive faculty member will be counseled by the academic chairperson. Second, if no improvement is exhibited, he or she will be criticized in writing by the academic chairperson. Third, and only in unusual situations, the faculty member will be penalized financially, at the direction of the university administration.

In general terms, the motivation for faculty members to be productive is described as follows. The motivation for younger faculty members is to move up within the academic ranks of the department. This can be achieved by teaching extra courses and serving on committees within the university. Research productivity is more of a consideration in some of the positions. The benefits of such efforts include better housing, higher pay, and aspirations for promotion.

The motivation for older faculty members is a major problem. With pay levels fixed, faculty who have reached higher levels of seniority tend to seek money from sources outside the university. If they can work outside of the university and not have it reported to the university, they can keep all the money. If the university knows of the employment it will receive up to 50% of the additional salary. Thus, older faculty members will generally try to teach as little as possible in the university but work as much as possible (off the record) outside of the university. Thus, junior faculty members tend to shoulder more duties within the academic departments.

Promotion of faculty is approved by a research group committee in each department. This committee is comprised of four senior ranking department members. The request for promotion is initiated by the research group committee, and "rubber stamp" approval generally follows from the university promotion committee and the Ministry of Railway, which governs Northern Jiaotong University.

I readily observed such processes during my periods of teaching at Northern Jiaotong University. By U.S. standards it would seem junior faculty would resent this process, but, on the contrary, junior faculty will someday be able to enjoy certain liberties when they are senior faculty.

This situation is obviously a problem for academic chairpersons. They have control over faculty members' well-being within the academic department but little, if any, control over faculty pay and termination.

In another area, faculty governance by faculty and academic chairpersons is far less existent compared with the U.S. Zhao Yuguang (not his real name) reports that he feels frustrated by restrictions on faculty participation in academic decision making. They are free to express opinions when "alone in the classroom" with students, but he reports they have "virtually no say in departmental affairs." He says there is no discussion at university meetings. "There is a speaker. I only have to bring my ears" (Jacobsen, November 4, 1987, p. A-48).

The impact of the cultural revolution (1966-1976) on higher education in China cannot be overstated. It seems to provide a constant referent in China's educational development. One will hear "because of the cultural revolution..., before the cultural revolution..., since the cultural revolution..., or during the cultural revolution...." (Jacobsen, November 4, 1987, p. A-49). Due to its recency, the cultural revolution has affected everyone at all levels of higher education in China. As time passes perhaps the effects of the cultural revolution, and the persecution of higher education, will diminish.

It is imperative to consider the role of politics in Chinese universities and Chinese society overall. Department chairpersons must consistently consider concerns stressed directly (and indirectly) by the government. Communist Party officials exercise considerable influence upon the day-to-day operations within Chinese universities. A department chairperson that is out of step with political concerns of the government jeopardizes his or her position. The benefits that come with the chairperson position (i.e., better living conditions, travel, telephone service, etc.) are also in jeopardy. These benefits are an important incentive because the salaries are so low that most faculty members cannot afford more than basic necessities. For instance, the typical Chinese faculty member does not have a home telephone.

Thus, issues such as curriculum development are carried out with a sensitivity toward the political climate. The U.S. political system affords academics (and those that manage them) far more autonomy with curriculum development. The divide between the U.S. and Chinese educational systems is so wide in this area that it is difficult to fully convey the role of "political correctness" in the functioning of academic departments. Any formal subject matter that contradicts the views of the Chinese government will draw a negative response from the government.

The closest parallel to which the situation can be related is that of the free press in the U.S. Private newspapers exercise considerable freedom in what they publish (as universities in the U.S. exercise considerable freedom in what they teach). There is a stark comparison, however, when independent newspapers are compared with base newspapers on military installations (I am a military reservist and have had exposure to such publications). Base newspapers are published by, for, about and in support of the military mission (as course content in China is intended to be in support of its "revolutionary struggle"). The base newspaper editor who prints stories contradicting the goals of the installation will not be editor very long (just as the academic chairperson who allows the teaching of course content that opposes government views will not be chairperson very long). This situation does not require an extensive list of do's and don'ts. The basic guidelines are "don't rock the boat" and "stay in line."

The political influences that affect curriculum development affect the functioning of departments overall. The curriculum development situation merely exemplifies the role of politics. Thus, departmental decision making, duties of department members, teaching assignments, and departmental governance are guided by a balancing act between what is the logical solution to an issue and what are the political ramifications.

I observed "fine lines" that one can sense and get close to, but should not cross. For example, in the spring of 1993 I taught a seminar series at a university in Beijing on political rhetoric. This seminar series, by coincidence, coincided with the anniversary of the 1989 pro-democracy movement and subsequent crackdown on dissent in China. My visits to China have given me an appreciation of what is politically appropriate and inappropriate. My sense was that it would be okay to lecture on political rhetoric concepts but not use the situation in China as an example (though it exemplified the seminar content quite well). To cross that line, using China as an example, might hinder future invitations to visit the university.

Although, I was not told what to teach I believed that future invitations to visit the university were contingent upon my not criticizing the government, so I did not explicitly acknowledge the situation in China one way or the other. Informal conversations with students attending the seminar series led me to believe that attendees made desired connections between rhetorical theory concepts and reality in China that I chose not to state explicitly. If a foreigner can sense these "fine lines," native Chinese certainly have a heightened awareness of them and an ability to function within them. I am interested to see if the aforementioned functioning of departments mentioned earlier changes significantly as reforms in China are implemented.

The Chinese educational system and the society as a whole are developing rapidly. As international exchanges continue to occur with the United States, in the private and academic sectors, I am optimistic regarding the benefits that can be realized by both countries. China is adopting many of our technologies and practices. The U.S. is able to learn from Chinese successes and failures. The much heralded global economy of the future will no doubt be built upon global understanding today. This chapter is intended as a contribution to that understanding.

References

Cross, D.E., Baker, G.C., and Stiles, L.J., eds. *Teaching in a Multicultural Society.* New York: The Free Press, 1981.

Culturegrams: The Nations around Us. Volume I and Volume II. The Center for International Studies, Brigham Young University. Yarmouth: Intercultural Press, 1987.

Hofstede, G. *Culture's Consequences: International Differences in Work Related Values.* Beverly Hills: Sage Publications, 1980.

Jacobsen, R.L. "China's Campuses: Life Today May Often be a Struggle, but Few Forget the Tougher Times Not Long Ago," *Chronicle of Higher Education* (November 4, 1987) pp. A48-52.

_____. "Expectations Rise for Higher Education in China as Reform Temper Begins to Take Hold," *Chronicle of Higher Education* (October 28, 1987) pp. 40-42.

Li Xing, "Teachers to Play Social Roles," *China Daily* (April 27, 1987) p. 3.

Mote, F.W. *The Intellectual Foundations of China.* New York: Alfred A. Knopf, 1971.

Roberts, K.H., and Boyacigiller, N. "Research Review: A Survey of Cross-national Organizational Researchers: Their Views and Opinions." *Organizational Studies*, Vol. 4 (1983) pp. 375-386.

Yang Chuanwei, "Stepping up Teachers' Training," *China Daily* (May 26, 1987), p. 4.

Chapter Nine

Intercultural Communication Education
in the People's Republic of China

The purpose of this chapter is to describe how the Chinese educational system promotes intercultural communication education. The Chinese approach differs from approaches in the United States, as intercultural communication education is promoted primarily through English teacher education programs. Since the opening of China, the teaching of English has been a priority in Chinese education. Students are taught not only the English language, but they are also taught about the cultures and ethnic groups who are native speakers of English. Thus, the English language and English speaking cultures are simultaneously emphasized in English teacher training. This approach provides intercultural understanding of both language and culture.

This chapter is primarily based on intercultural communication education practices at Northern Jiaotong University in Beijing, the People's Republic of China. I taught students who were being trained to be English teachers, observed the English teacher training process at various levels, and formally surveyed student perceptions of their English teacher training.

Teacher education in the People's Republic of China has parallels with teacher education in the United States but it also has marked differences. A primary difference deals with the greater emphasis the Chinese give to intercultural communication. The teacher education processes used there are based on the unique development of the country.

In 1979, an open door policy was implemented in an effort to help China compete with the outside world. Since that time, trade and joint business ventures with the west have been emphasized strongly, specifically with the United States. China is eager to open to the outside world, but only on its own terms. The following excerpt provides a description of these terms.

Closing one's country to external contact results only in stagnation and backwardness. We resolutely reject the capitalist ideological and social systems that defend oppression and exploitation, and we reject all the ugly and decadent aspects of capitalism. Nevertheless, we should do our utmost to learn from all countries. . . .

Otherwise, we shall remain ignorant and be unable to modernize our own country. ("Resolution of the Central Committee...," 1986, p. 6)

As interaction with the United States increases, so does the demand for English language training. "China still has a long way to go in making its population fully literate in Chinese, let alone in English. But in terms of both national goals and individual aspirations, English is near the top of the list" (Jacobsen, Oct. 28, 1987). English is now taught widely at all levels of education within China. By the time students of English reach the high school level they have normally had at least three years of English language training and, during the high school period, are expected to achieve a conversational ability with the English language. "In the universities, students practice English with a passion that comes from knowing where the future lies" (Jacobsen, Oct. 28, 1987).

Students are trained to gain an understanding of English speaking cultures as they study the English language. The government wants students to learn not only the English language but to learn about the people who speak the English language. Thus, intercultural communication in China is promoted through emphasis on English teacher education programs.

This approach minimizes a problem that has existed in the teaching of English in China and other countries, that is, students can learn the English vocabulary but have difficulty in communicating and understanding conceptual meanings. "Lack of competent English teachers and under- estimation of the lesson time that should be devoted to verbal comprehension and speaking in English were mainly responsible for students' low performance in learning English." "The poor English ability of middle school students is a potential obstacle to the country's opening to the outside world" ("Students Found Poor....," 1987). An official government objective, such as the opening of China, is taken very seriously by the Chinese people. Thus, answers to such problems are actively sought.

In teaching English as a second language, the emphasis on the communication process cannot be overstated. Dorothy Bainton, chairperson of the Pathology Department at the University of California at San Francisco, conducts a two week workshop to prepare Chinese health care workers who will be studying in the U.S. "Even though they may read English quite well, they may have difficulty understanding the spoken language and making themselves understood. And they face the broader problem of conflicting rules about communication and socialization" (Jacobsen, Nov. 4, 1987).

These barriers to effective interaction are grounded in intercultural communication differences. Intercultural communication "occurs when two or more individuals with different cultural backgrounds interact together. . . . In most situations intercultural interactants do not share the same language. But languages can be learned and larger communication problems occur in the nonverbal realm" (Andersen, 1986, p. 88). "Since we are not usually aware of our own nonverbal behavior it becomes extremely difficult to identify and master the nonverbal behavior of another culture. At times we feel uncomfortable in other cultures because we intuitively know something isn't right" (Andersen, 1987, pp. 2-3). "Because nonverbal behaviors are rarely conscious phenomena, it may be difficult for us to know exactly why we are feeling uncomfortable" (Gudykunst and Kim, 1984, p. 149). The intercultural obstacles to effective listening exist in a similar manner.

The effect of the cultural backgrounds of interactants on human interaction is a crucial consideration. "Culture is the enduring influence of the social environment on our behavior including our interpersonal communication behaviors" (Andersen, 1987, p. 6). The culture of an individual dictates interpersonal behavior through "control mechanisms—plans, recipes, rules, instructions (what computer engineers call programs)—for the governing of behavior" (Geertz, 1973, p. 44). Thus, the process for presentation of ideas (speaking) and the reception of ideas (listening) will understandably vary from culture to culture.

A written survey of seven questions was administered to an English class of twenty students. These students were freshmen in the teacher preparation program at Northern Jiaotong University. They were requested to respond to seven statements (SA — strongly agree, A — agree, N — neutral, D— disagree, or SD — strongly disagree). The purpose of the survey was to study their perceptions of the role of communication in the teaching process. Results of the survey are as follows.

1. I think I will be a good teacher of English.

SA	A	N	D	SD
85%	5%	—	10%	—

2. I will most likely work as a teacher until I retire.

SA	A	N	D	SD
20%	25%	20%	35%	—

3. Teaching English is more difficult than teaching other foreign languages.

SA	A	N	D	SD
5%	15%	30%	45%	5%

4. As an English teacher, my behavior will serve as an important role model for my students (regarding social responsibility).

SA	A	N	D	SD
35%	45%	15%	5%	—

5. Intellectual development is more important than moral education and physical education.

SA	A	N	D	SD
10%	55%	25%	5%	5%

6. Teaching English was my first choice over other types of jobs.

SA	A	N	D	SD
20%	20%	—	35%	25%

7. Sometimes I understand the words an English speaker is using, but I don't understand his or her main idea or message.

SA	A	N	D	SD
15%	50%	10%	25%	—

For the purpose of this chapter I am most concerned with questions four, six, and seven.

Question four responses indicate that most students feel their behavior will serve as an important role model for students (regarding social responsibility). Eighty percent agreed (or strongly agreed) with this statement, compared with five percent who disagreed. This corresponds with a statement made by Li Peng, former Minister of the State Education Commission, regarding teachers serving as role models. "Schools in China should be most concerned with turning out youngsters with high ideals . . . and a devotion to socialism. . . . Faculty members should improve themselves by mastering Marxist theory, the Communist Party's principles and academic knowledge" (Xing, 1987, p. 1). Li Peng is presently the Premier of China.

Question six responses show that less than half of the students selected teaching English as their first choice of occupations. Sixty percent said teaching English was not their first choice, while 40% said teaching English was their first choice. I cannot speculate why there is such a high percentage of reluctant teachers, but I feel it is worth noting.

Question seven responses indicate that 65% of the students agree or strongly agree that they sometimes understand the words an English speaker is using but don't understand his or her main ideas or message. Twenty-five percent disagreed with this statement.

The survey has shortcomings. Twenty students is a limited number from which to draw thorough conclusions. The questions do not directly address intercultural communication. However, collection of accurate survey data in an oppressive society such as China is very difficult. This survey does provide a glimpse and context for the topic of this chapter.

A variety of techniques is incorporated in coursework to meet the intercultural communication education objective. The Chinese have used the "Follow Me" English language videotape instruction series to teach English language and British culture. The series includes over 48 one hour segments that instruct the student on English language comprehension and how the language fits within the context of British society. Many archetypal aspects of British culture are consistently emphasized throughout the series. I found that when I taught English using the "Follow Me" series, Chinese students concurrently learned a great deal about British culture.

Similarly, I was encouraged by senior Chinese colleagues to describe U.S. culture as context for English language usage. Chinese students are interested in learning about the U.S., so the instructor can productively intertwine English language instruction with American norms and folkways. For instance, to explain the continual evolution of the American English language I correlated the constant change of the language with the constant change of the American culture. This led to many examples of American slang and descriptions of how slang terms (i.e., rock and roll, Reaganomics, fuzz-buster, etc.) evolve. Students correctly learn to associate American culture with change.

This approach correlates bilingualism with biculturalism. In *Communicating with China*, interpreter Jan Carol Berris states, "Biculturalism—sensitivity to cultural and social differences—is often as important as bilingualism" (Berris, 1983, p. 42).

When an individual becomes bicultural he or she goes through an acculturation process as the new culture is learned. "Acculturation occurs through the identification and the internalization of the significant symbols of the host society" (Kim, 1988, p. 345). Young Yun Kim, in "Communication and Acculturation," emphasizes personal and social communication within acculturation. "Personal (or intrapersonal) communication refers to the mental processes by which one organizes oneself in and with one's sociocultural milieu, developing ways of seeing, hearing, understanding and responding to the environment" (Kim, 1988, p. 346). "Through social communication, individuals regulate feelings, thoughts, and actions of one another" (Kim, 1988, p. 347). Social communication is the interpersonal application of each person's personal communication basis of understanding.

Kim sees ethnicity and acculturation as being interrelated. "When the changes (to a new culture) are not complete, it is only natural that there remains a certain degree of ethnicity. Incomplete acculturation, depending on one's point of view, can be interpreted as evidence of (some) assimilation or (some) ethnicity" (Kim, 1988, p. 350).

Ethnicity can be described through the definition of ethnic groups offered by Albert and Triandis. "To the extent that ethnic groups have characteristic ways of behaving, they exhibit somewhat different distributions of behavior configurations. . . . An ethnic group, then, may consist of individuals having characteristic behavior patterns and subjective cultures" (Albert and Triandis, 1985, p. 392).

The educational system in China seeks to promote intercultural communication education through emphasis on English teacher education. Practitioners offer three primary approaches for achieving this objective: the experiential, behavioral, and informational approaches.

The experiential method involves the learner actually experiencing the culture by living there for a period of time. Since this is not usually feasible, especially with Chinese learners, there are other diluted approaches within the experiential method. This would include creating laboratory or "imitation" cultural settings or spending time visiting ethnic neighborhoods which practice perspectives of the studied culture (Albert and Triandis, 1985, p. 397).

The behavioral method involves "reinforcing the individual for producing behavioral patterns which are commonly found in another culture" (Albert and Triandis, 1985, p. 397). The goal is to teach individuals about another culture rather than to change behavior. Similarly, Kim suggests acculturation can be effectively achieved "through communication training programs. Such training programs should facilitate the immigrants' acquisition of the host communication competence" (Kim, 1988, p. 350).

The third, and most common, approach is the informational method, which focuses on readings about other peoples' customs or history (Albert and Triandis, 1985, p. 397). This method seeks to provide a perspective or context within which the culture operates. Barna suggests studying the history, political structure, art, literature and language of the new culture (Barna, 1988, p. 325). This, again, encourages the learner to understand the framework of the culture rather than specific behaviors which are offensive or complimentary.

Similarly, Stewart warns against studying a list of "do's and don'ts," since behavior is ambiguous (depending on the situations and circumstances encountered). He stresses that the learner consider his or her own behavior and how it is affected by his or her assumptions and values (Stewart, 1972, p. 20). Assumptions and values vary from culture to culture, thus it is a stumbling block to "assume similarity instead of difference" when interpreting situations in a new culture (Barna, 1988, p. 375).

Triandis suggests the use of attribution training within the informational method. This technique "aims to teach members of one culture to make attributions commonly made by members of another culture. Attributions are interpretations of behavior; that is, they are inferences about the causes of a given behavior" (Triandis, 1975, pp. 69-77). This is helpful since attributions are based on norms, roles, affects, and consequences of actions which are operating in a particular situation (Triandis, 1975, pp. 69-77).

I concur with the position offered by Triandis that attribution training should be emphasized within the informational method. Since the 1989 pro-democracy movement in China, student interest in learning about democracy has increased considerably. Use of this motivation to learn about the U.S. (a democracy) provides a useful means for teaching English, as it is couched in the norms, roles, affects and consequences of actions that operate in the U.S. Thus, the Chinese student effectively learns the language, how it is used, and with what effects. Ideally, the student can work toward speaking and thinking American English.

As the People's Republic of China opens to the outside world, the learning of English continues to be an important objective in its educational system. Its experience has shown that it is not enough to merely teach the English language, rather, it is also important to teach about the cultures within which the English language is spoken, as this provides a context for language usage. Teachers are being trained in large numbers to teach English to Chinese students. In meeting this goal, China is emphasizing intercultural communication education within its English teacher preparation programs.

References

Albert, R.D., and Triandis, H.C. "Intercultural Education for Multicultural Societies: Critical Issues," *International Journal of Intercultural Relations 9* (1985).

Andersen, P.A. "Explaining Intercultural Differences in Nonverbal Communication." Paper presented at the annual meeting of the Speech Communication Association (Boston, MA), November 1987.

_____. "Consciousness, Cognition, and Communication," *Western Journal of Speech Communication 50* (1986).

Barna, L.M. "Stumbling Blocks in Intercultural Communication." In Samovar, L.A., and Porter, R.E. *Intercultural Communication: A Reader.* Belmont, CA: Wadsworth Publishing Co., 1988.

Berris, J.C. "The Art of Interpreting." In Kapp, R.A. (ed.), *Communicating with China.* Chicago: Intercultural Press, 1983.

Geertz, C. *The Interpretation of Cultures*. New York: Basic Books, 1973.
Gudykunst, W.B., and Kim, Y.Y. *Communicating with Strangers: An Approach to Intercultural Communication*. New York: Random House, 1984.
Jacobsen, R.L. "Expectations Rise for Higher Education in China as Reform Temper Begins to Take Hold," *Chronicle of Higher Education* (October 28, 1987).
_____. "Workshop Helps Chinese Prepare for U.S.," *Chronicle of Higher Education* (November 4, 1987).
Kim, Y.Y. "Communication and Acculturation." In Samovar, L.A., and Porter, R.E. *Intercultural Communication: A Reader*. Belmont, CA: Wadsworth Publishing Co., 1988.
Resolution of the Central Committee of the CPC on the Guiding Principles for Building a Socialist Society with an Advanced Culture and Ideology. Foreign Language Press: Beijing, The People's Republic of China (September 1986).
Stewart, E.C. *American Cultural Patterns: A Cross-Cultural Perspective*. 906 N. Spring Ave., LaGrange Park, Illinois 60525: Intercultural Network, Inc., 1972.
"Students Found Poor in English," *China Daily* (May 2, 1987).
Triandis, H.C. "Training, Cognitive Complexity, and Interpersonal Attitudes." In Brislin, R.W., Bochner, S., and Lonner, W. (eds.), *Cross-Cultural Perspectives on Learning*. New York: Halsted/Wiley/Sage, 1975.
Xing, L. "Li Stresses Civic Role of Schools," *China Daily* (May 4, 1987).

Chapter Ten

The Need for Listening Theory
When Teaching English as a Second Language

Since World War II, there has been a dramatic increase in world trade. This increase has also involved a variety of other developments promoting international interaction. One such development is that English has become a predominant language in the international community, and the teaching of English, to non-native speakers, has become common all over the world.

During the spring term (March-June) 1987, when I was a visiting professor at Northern Jiaotong University in Beijing I taught English as a second language to native Chinese speakers. This gave me the opportunity to work with a team of faculty members, teaching the same course, and the chance to research the process of teaching English as a second language.

Since the opening of China in 1979, the learning of English has been emphasized strongly. "China still has a long way to go in making its population fully literate in Chinese, let alone in English. But in terms of both national goals and individual aspirations, English is near the top of the list" (Jacobsen, October 28, 1987, p. 40).

The teaching of English is done, to a considerable degree, outside of the traditional classroom. "Lessons also are broadcast on national radio every day" (Jacobsen, October 28, 1987, p. A40). Thus, the implications for the distant learner in this process are strong. "Nearly two million people are now following satellite T.V. education programs in their spare time, according to the State Education Commission" ("T.V. Education," 1987).

An article entitled "T.V. Series to Help Kids Learn English" described a "new T.V. series to help Chinese children in primary schools to learn English" (*China Daily*, May 1, 1987). Entitled "Let's Learn English," the program is a response to the shortage of qualified English teachers in China.

The teaching of English in China, in the classroom and with distant learner approaches, has had its problems. A common problem is that students can learn the English vocabulary but have difficulty in communicating and understanding conceptual meanings.

During my teaching assignment in China, I perceived student comprehension of English language vocabulary to be far better than their ability to communicate their ideas and understand the ideas of others. Based upon my experience, I hypothesized that their comprehension of factual information is good but their comprehension of main ideas is deficient. Observation of, and discussion with, other teachers evidenced a curriculum which contained no emphasis on the importance of listening skills in the communication process. Thus, students were primarily taught words and expressions but were not taught about communicating or interpreting main ideas properly. The latter seemed to be assumed.

A written survey of six questions was administered to an English class of twenty students. These students were freshmen in the teacher preparation program at Northern Jiaotong University. They were requested to respond to six statements (SA — strongly agree, A — agree, N — neutral, D — disagree, or SD — strongly disagree). The purpose of the survey was to study their perceptions of the role of listening in the communication process. Results of the survey are as follows.

1. I have received a lot of practice in the testing of my English listening skills.

SA	A	N	D	SD
20%	30%	5%	35%	10%

2. My English listening skills are good.

SA	A	N	D	SD
—	20%	40%	30%	10%

3. Sometimes I understand the words an English speaker is using, but I don't understand his or her main idea or message.

SA	A	N	D	SD
15%	50%	10%	25%	—

4. Hearing is the same as listening.

SA	A	N	D	SD
—	10%	25%	45%	20%

5. The most common distraction I experience when listening to an English speaker is noise which results in me not being able to hear him or her (such as noise from other students or noise in the hallway).

SA	A	N	D	SD
—	35%	45%	20%	—

6. When I am listening, the feedback I give to a speaker affects his or her message.

SA	A	N	D	SD
—	40%	25%	35%	—

The survey responses indicate a lack of understanding of the role of listening. For the purpose of this chapter, I am most concerned with questions three, four, and six.

Question three responses show that students believe they have a good understanding of English vocabulary but have problems with understanding a speaker's main ideas. Sixty-five percent agreed (or strongly agreed) with this statement, compared with 25 percent who disagreed with this statement.

Question four responses relate that students understand there is a difference between hearing and listening. Only ten percent felt there was no difference between hearing and listening.

Question six responses indicate that students need instruction on the role of feedback in the listening process. Only 40 percent agreed that listener feedback affects the speaker's message.

The survey results do not reveal a major void in student understanding of the role of listening in human interaction, but the need for more emphasis on listening is evident. When linked with the deficiencies described in newspaper and journal accounts of English education in China, a pattern of how English is taught begins to emerge. It is my contention that this process achieves the basic objective of teaching vocabulary, but more emphasis on the communication process, in this case listening, would enhance student understanding considerably. It is worth noting that other cross-cultural communication differences also exist within the learning of English.

The implications of high and low context communication processes, across cultures, provides another example of the effect of culture on the listening process. "A high-context communication or message is one in which most of the information is either in the physical context or internalized in the person, while very little is in the coded, explicit, transmitted parts of the message" (Hall, 1976, p. 91). For instance, people who know each other very well can communicate through unexplicit messages which are not readily understandable to a third party. "In high context situations or cultures information is integrated from the environment, the context, the situation, and from nonverbal cues that give the message meaning unavailable in the explicit verbal utterance" (Andersen, 1987, p. 22).

Low context messages (and cultures) are just the opposite of high context messages; most of the information is in the explicit code (Hall, 1976). Low context messages must be elaborated, clearly communicated, and highly specific (Andersen, 1987, p. 22). The lowest context cultures are probably Swiss, German, North American (including the U.S.) and Scandinavian (Hall, 1976; Gudykunst and Kim, 1984). These cultures are preoccupied with specifics, details, and precise time schedules at the expense of context (Andersen, 1987, p. 22).

The highest context cultures are found in the Orient. China, Japan, and Korea are very high context cultures (Elliot, Scott, Jensen and McDonough, 1982; Hall, 1976). "Languages are some of the most explicit communication systems but the Chinese language is an implicit high context system" (Andersen, 1987, p. 23). Americans (from a low context culture) will complain that Japanese (from a high context culture) never "get to the point." This is due to a failure to recognize that high context cultures must provide a context and setting and let the point evolve (Hall, 1984).

People in high context cultures expect more than interactants in low context cultures (Hall, 1976). Such expectations assume that the other person will "understand unarticulated feelings, subtle gestures and environmental clues that people from low context cultures simply do not process. Worse, both cultural extremes fail to recognize these basic differences in behavior, communication, and context and are quick to misattribute the causes for their behaviors" (Andersen, 1987, p. 25). Thus, awareness of influences on the listening process can have direct benefits for the Chinese person (high context) learning English (low context) as a second language.

I suggest, as a minimum, the teaching of theoretical considerations which can enhance understanding of the listening process. Emphasis on general ideas rather than specific skills can be helpful, depending on the learning situation, as awareness is the first step to overcoming listening barriers. Emphasis on listening distractions, listening distortions, criteria affecting listener response, and active listening would provide a relevant awareness of common problems in the listening process.

Four listening distractions detail some basic obstacles we frequently encounter in listening. Factual distractions occur when we listen for facts instead of main ideas. Semantic distractions occur when words or phrases are used differently (when one word has various meanings or one meaning has various words). Mental distractions occur when we have intrapersonal communication while engaged in interpersonal communication (i.e., daydreaming). Physical distractions are merely stimuli in the environment, such as noise (Devito, p. 329).

Three bases of listening distortion describe other fundamental considerations which can improve effective listening efforts. First, meaning is not transmitted in oral communication; only aural and visual stimuli are transmitted. Thus, meanings that listeners attach to messages are based on inferences instead of facts. Second, listening is a form of intrapersonal communication. That is, we reflect on the meaning of what is said to us. Third, listener expectations affect what is heard and comprehended. It is helpful to remember that a single message can be interpreted differently depending on the expectations of the listener (Barker, p. 78).

There are four primary criteria which affect listener response to a message. Listener "purpose" for attending to the message given will affect his or her response (i.e., once the purpose is met he or she may not listen anymore). Listener "knowledge of, and interest in, the subject" is based on his or her background and future goals. Listening "skills" involve the ability to follow ideas, recognize inferences, and detect deficiencies in evidence presented. Listener "attitudes" on the subject being discussed will affect the likelihood of support or rejection of the main premises. An example of this occurs when we are more easily swayed by views which align our own (Ehninger et al. pp. 211-212).

Active listening can be suggested as a general approach to effective listening. This approach involves listening to understand and provide feedback, not making strong judgments regarding speaker statements, listening for content (what is said) and feelings (how it is said), and restatement to ensure understanding (Devito, p. 243). Active listening is commonly used in counseling as a means to ensure listener understanding of the speaker's message and to promote effective feedback from the listener. The same guidelines can be used to aid understanding in everyday interactions.

The ideas presented in this chapter are relevant because the learning of a new language, whether or not it is English, involves considerable emphasis on the listening process. Although a person can learn the words of a new language, this does not prepare him or her to interact (both send and receive messages). Such a deficiency increases the likelihood of misunderstanding and ineffective interaction.

English as a second language is frequently taught to distant learners in the form of audio cassettes and written materials. The inclusion of listening instruction would not be difficult with such programs, and the desired objectives could be realistically met. I feel acknowledgment of the ideas presented in this chapter can substantially improve the teaching and learning of English as a second language. Specific applications would, of course, depend on the intended audience and the means used to convey information.

References

Andersen, P.A. "Consciousness, Cognition, and Communication," *Western Journal of Speech Communication* 50 (1986) pp. 87-101.

_____. "Explaining Intercultural Differences in Nonverbal Communication." Paper presented at the annual meeting of the Speech Communication Association (Boston, MA), November 1987.

Barker, L. *Listening Behavior*. New York: Prentice-Hall, 1973.

Devito, J. *The Interpersonal Communication Book*. New York: Wm. C. Brown, 1986.

Ehninger, D., Gronbeck, B., McKerrow, R., and Monroe, A. *Principles and Types of Speech Communication*. New York: Scott, Foresman, and Co., 1986.

Elliot, S., Scott, M.D., Jensen, A.D., and McDonough, M. "Perceptions of Reticence: A Cross-Cultural Investigation." In M. Burgoon (Ed.), *Communication Yearbook 5* (pp. 591-602). New Brunswick, New Jersey: Transaction Books, 1982.

Geertz, C. *The Interpretation of Cultures*. New York: Basic Books, 1973.

Gudykunst, W.B., and Kim, Y.Y. *Communicating with Strangers: An Approach to Intercultural Communication*. New York: Random House, 1984.

Hall, E.T. *Beyond Culture*. Garden City, New York: Anchor Books, 1976.

_____. *The Dance of Life: The Other Dimension of Time*. Garden City, New York: Anchor Books, 1984.

Jacobsen, R.L. 'Expectations Rise for Higher Education in China as Reform Temper Begins to Take Hold," *Chronicle of Higher Education* (October 28, 1987), pp. A40-42.

_____. "Workshop Helps Chinese Prepare for U.S.," *Chronicle of Higher Education* (November 4, 1987), p. A49.

"Students Found Poor in English," *China Daily* (May 2, 1987), p. 3.

"T.V. Education," *China Daily* (May 15, 1987), p. 3.

"T.V. Series to Help Kids Learn English," *China Daily* (May 1, 1987), p. 5.

Chapter Eleven

The Need for Nonverbal Communication Theory
When Teaching English as a Second Language

During the spring term (March-June) 1987, when I was a visiting professor at Northern Jiaotong University in Beijing, I taught English as a second language to native Chinese speakers. This gave me the opportunity to work with a team of faculty members, teaching the same course, and the chance to research the process of teaching English as a second language.

During my teaching assignment in China, I perceived student comprehension of English language vocabulary to be far better than their ability to communicate their ideas and understand the ideas of others. Based upon my experience, I hypothesized that their comprehension of factual information is good but their comprehension of main ideas is deficient. Observation of, and discussion with, other teachers evidenced a curriculum that contained no emphasis on the importance of nonverbal communication skills in the communication process. Thus, students were primarily taught words and expressions but were not taught about communicating or interpreting ideas. The latter seemed to be assumed.

A written survey of six questions was administered to an English class of twenty students. These students were freshmen in the teacher preparation program at Northern Jiaotong University. They were requested to respond to six statements (SA — strongly agree, A — agree, N — neutral, D — disagree, or SD — strongly disagree). The purpose of the survey was to study their perceptions of
the role of nonverbal communication in the communication process. Results of the survey are as follows.

1. Verbal communication carries more meaning with a message than non-verbal communication.

SA	A	N	D	SD
10%	20%	35%	30%	5%

2. Native speakers of English are more expressive nonverbally (i.e., gesture more) than are native Chinese people.

SA   A   N   D   SD
—   30%   50%   10%   10%

3. I tend to be more expressive nonverbally when I'm speaking English than
when I'm speaking Chinese.
SA   A   N   D   SD
10%   45%   15%   30%   —

4. American nonverbal communication is different than British nonverbal
communication.
SA   A   N   D   SD
10%   45%   35%   10%   —

5. American nonverbal communication is different than Chinese nonverbal
communication.
SA   A   N   D   SD
25%   55%   5%   15%   —

6. I think I could communicate better in English if I learned more about nonverbal communication norms in English speaking countries.
SA   A   N   D   SD
50%   40%   5%   5%   —

The survey responses indicate a lack of understanding of nonverbal
communication processes. For the purpose of this chapter, I am most concerned
with questions three, five, and six.

Question three responses indicate that a little more than half of the students
feel they are more expressive nonverbally when they are speaking English than
when they are speaking Chinese. Fifty-five percent agreed with this statement,
while only 30 percent disagreed with the statement.

Question five responses show that most students feel American
nonverbal communication is different than Chinese nonverbal communication.
Eighty percent agreed with this statement and only 15 percent disagreed.

Question six responses demonstrate that a strong majority of the students feel
that they could communicate better in English if they learned more about
nonverbal communication norms in English speaking countries. Ninety percent
agreed with this point of view, and only five percent disagreed with the
statement.

The survey results do not reveal a major void in student understanding of the
role of nonverbal communication in human interaction, but the need for more

emphasis on nonverbal communication is evident. When linked with the deficiencies described in newspaper and journal accounts of English education in China, a pattern of how English is taught emerges. It is my contention that this process achieves the basic objective of teaching vocabulary, but more emphasis on the communication process, in this case nonverbal communication, will enhance student understanding considerably.

I suggest, as a minimum, the teaching of theoretical considerations which can enhance understanding of the nonverbal communication processes. Emphasis on general ideas rather than specific skills can be helpful, depending on the learning situation, as awareness is the first step to overcoming nonverbal barriers. Emphasis on proxemics, vocalics, kinesics, eye behavior, and tactile communication will help provide a relevant awareness of nonverbal communication processes.

At the outset, it is very important to stress that these nonverbal areas are relevant because the rules which govern these areas vary from culture to culture and language to language. Thus, when one travels to a foreign country one is exposed to a new verbal language and a new nonverbal code of behavior.

Proxemics is the study of physical space and how it is consciously used in our day to day interactions. This includes awareness of physical distances that interactants maintain, depending upon the purpose of the interaction (intimate, personal, social and public distances). Territoriality norms (how we maintain personal space) are also included in this area.

Vocalics deals with vocal cues such as rate, pitch, inflection, volume, quality and enunciation. These cues are important in the understanding of paralanguage in each culture. Paralanguage emphasizes not what is said but how it is said. Thus, meanings can vary significantly, depending on how statements are said.

Kinesics is the study of body language such as hand, arm, chest and leg movements. Some of the more common kinesic behaviors are emblems, regulators, and illustrators. Emblems are acts which have a direct verbal translation. Regulators maintain the back and forth nature of speaking and listening. Illustrators support what we are saying verbally.

Eye behavior and tactile communication (touching behavior) are also important considerations when learning new nonverbal codes of behavior. Eye behavior signals the nature of a relationship, and it monitors feedback from the other person. The location, amount, and intensity of tactile communication are culturally determined.

Again, it is a central premise that these nonverbal areas are important because the codes which govern each of these areas vary from culture to culture. Thus, if we are not sensitive to these considerations, our nonverbal messages can contradict or negatively affect our verbal message.

References

Andersen, P.A. "Consciousness, Cognition, and Communication," *Western Journal of Speech Communication*, 50 (1986) pp. 87-101.
_____. "Explaining Intercultural Differences in Nonverbal Communication." Paper presented at the annual meeting of the Speech Communication Association (Boston, MA), November 1987.
Devito, J. *The Interpersonal Communication Book*. New York: Wm. C. Brown, 1986.
Ehninger, D., Gronbeck, B., McKerrow, R. and Monroe, A. *Principles and Types of Speech Communication*. New York: Scott, Foresman, and Co., 1986.
Elliot, S., Scott, M.D., Jensen, A.D. and McDonough, M. "Perceptions of Reticence: A Cross-Cultural Investigation." In M. Burgoon (Ed.) *Communication Yearbook 5* (pp. 591-602). New Brunswick, New Jersey: Transaction Books, 1982.
Geertz, C. *The Interpretation of Cultures*. New York: Basic Books, 1973.
Gudykunst, W.B. and Kim, Y.Y. *Communicating with Strangers: An Approach to Intercultural Communication*. New York: Random House, 1984.
Hall, E.T. *Beyond Culture*. Garden City, New York: Anchor Books, 1976.
_____. *The Dance of Life: The Other Dimension of Time*. Garden City, New York: Anchor Books, 1984.
Jacobsen, R.L. "Expectations Rise for Higher Education in China as Reform Temper Begins to Take Hold," *Chronicle of Higher Education* (October 28, 1987), pp. A40-42.
_____. "Workshop Helps Chinese Prepare for U.S.", *Chronicle of Higher Education* (November 4, 1987), p. A49.
"Students Found Poor in English," *China Daily* (May 2, 1987), p. 3.
"T.V. Education," *China Daily* (May 15, 1987), p. 3.
"T.V. Series to Help Kids Learn English," *China Daily* (May 1, 1987), p. 5.

Chapter Twelve

The Developmental Speech Sequence Model
in Public Speaking Instruction

Developmental education has been used in a variety of disciplines in higher education (Ahrendt, 1987; Zehr, 1990). Application within the context of this chapter deals with public speaking instruction, but this application has parallels with other areas of instruction as well. This chapter emphasizes a developmental education approach used in the United States and the People's Republic of China.

At the outset, it is helpful to clarify differences between remedial versus developmental education. Roueche and Wheeler (1973, p. 223) state that the objective of remedial programs is to remove "student deficiencies in order that the student may enter a program in which he was previously ineligible." Developmental programs focus on "skills and attitudes and may not have anything to do with making a student eligible for another program."

Patricia Cross (1976, p. 31) builds on these in terms of purpose. "If the purpose of the program is to overcome deficiencies," the program is remedial. If the purpose of the program is to "develop the diverse talents of students, whether academic or not . . .," it is a developmental program. In more general terms, according to the National Association for Developmental Education, developmental education is a "professional specialty concerned with promoting educational opportunity, academic skills development, and educational efficiency in postsecondary education" (Boylan, 1983, p. 5).

The emphasis of this chapter, regarding these two approaches, is on developmental programming in public speaking instruction. Much of the research for this chapter has been drawn from areas outside of public speaking instruction (i.e., math, English, and language instruction) and thus should have relevance with other disciplines.

Developmental education has been emphasized and studied in a variety of academic settings. Such analysis has served to better define the role of developmental education. Roueche and Snow (1977, p. 18) described and compared developmental programs in two and four year colleges. Their objective was to "shed light on the characteristics of highly successful programs" and to "discover what is being done and how well it is being done."

Roueche and Snow (1977, pp. 113-130) summarized and synthesized their findings with similar research efforts and found three general areas which are central to the developmental education process: 1) the teacher is the key, 2) supportive services are vital for success, and 3) proper organizational support is essential for effective programs.

I am concerned with the first area, the teacher is the key. The teacher is the most influential aspect of the developmental process since she or he decides what is to be learned. "Content selection can be the most powerful incentive to student motivation and significant learning" (Roueche and Snow, 1977, p. 114). Another important decision made by the teacher is how the subject matter will be taught. Students should know what is expected of them.

There is overwhelming acknowledgment of the importance of teachers being genuinely concerned with their students as human beings (Lehr, 1988; Shapiro, 1989; Roueche and Baker, 1987). Learning student names exemplifies an approach in this area, that is, showing interest in them as people, not just as students. "Good human involvement with learners was a real key to getting students motivated and trying in college" (Roueche and Snow, 1977, p. 120).

Regarding actual instructional practices within developmental programs, Roueche and Snow (1977) stress that instructional methods must be systematic in concept.

> Instructional methods should be built around developmental notions of sequencing the curriculum from the most simple behavioral objectives. . . . Instructional objectives which specify what the student will be able to do, under what conditions, and at what criterion level are the heart of instructional clarity. (p. 127)

I recognize the terms developmental and sequencing to be especially important, because the successful application of a developmental approach rests on effective sequencing.

As a professor of speech, I have used the developmental education approach to construct a model for use by my public speaking students. I have used a variety of models for teaching public speaking and have successfully used this model for the past fifteen years. The Developmental Speech Sequence Model (DSSM), named this by me because of its developmental approach, offers students guidelines for speech delivery but does not inhibit creativity.

There are four factors affecting student learning: 1) the student's ability to act, 2) the psychological-social learning situation, 3) a payoff, and 4) the student's evaluation of the payoff (Roueche and Snow, pp. 117-118). These factors are addressed by the DSSM. The student's ability to act is addressed by using basic behavioral objectives as building blocks for each assignment. The psychological-social learning situation is enhanced as students learn by doing amongst their peers. The payoff is the learning (or improvement) of a practical skill. Student evaluation of the payoff should be positive if they perceive themselves as learning (or improving) a practical skill.

I have modified the DSSM several times since I initially developed it. Changes have been based on student abilities to present speeches using this approach. I have found the model to be beneficial, as students know what is expected of them and they can develop their speeches in a variety of ways, depending on their individual skills and interests. Thus, when used in conjunction with stated objectives and classroom discussion of primary considerations, the DSSM can be applied with students who have varied abilities, strengths, and weaknesses.

There are many types of textbooks and approaches that profess a variety of ways to teach public speaking. Some approaches provide step-by-step direction, while others are more abstract. The DSSM is beneficial because it builds developmentally through a series of sequential phases. This approach is appropriate for the teaching of any type of self expression.

Northern Jiaotong University, like many other schools in China, emphasizes technical education. I have taught English and public speaking during my visits. This teaching assignment provided an opportunity to test the effectiveness of the DSSM with students in a foreign culture. I was particularly interested in using the DSSM in China, as it allowed me to gauge the flexibility of the model.

Two primary speeches in the basic public speaking course are the speech to inform and the speech to persuade. The DSSM can be used as a model for both of these speeches. The objective in using the DSSM is to give the students coherent guidelines to prepare their speeches but not at the expense of creativity.

The following provides a Speech to Inform outline using the DSSM.

INTRODUCTION

  I. OPENING ("Good afternoon. My name is . . .")
  II. OBJECTIVE OF SPEECH ("The objective of my speech to inform is to
    inform you . . .")
  III. OVERVIEW ("The main points I will cover in my speech to inform
    are . . .")

BODY

IV. CLARIFY IMPORTANCE OF TOPIC (Why should the audience be

interested in your topic?)
V. MAIN IDEA: INFORM THE AUDIENCE ABOUT YOUR TOPIC (This
is the main part of your speech.)
VI. STATEMENT OF SOURCES (Tell the audience the primary sources of
information you used in preparing your speech. How do you know what you
know about the topic?)
VII. SOURCES THE AUDIENCE CAN REFER TO (How can the audience
learn more about your topic?)

CONCLUSION

VIII. REVIEW ("The main points I have covered in my speech to inform
are . . .")
IX. RESTATEMENT OF OBJECTIVE ("The objective of my speech to
inform has been to inform you . . .")
X. CLOSING

The instructor should stress that students must address these ten areas in their
speech. Student response to this model is favorable because it takes the
guesswork out of their planning and answers the question, "What does the
instructor really want me to do?"

The line between adequate guidance and not inhibiting creativity is a fine one.
I view the DSSM as scaffolding (an organizational framework) upon which
students can hang their ideas. The intent is not to instruct students on what to say
but to instruct them on how to organize their content. A long term objective of
using the DSSM is that the student will internalize the conceptual framework
(main idea) of the DSSM and use this conceptual framework in out-of-class
settings. For instance, if the student is giving an informative presentation in a
work setting, about his or her function in the organization, she or he could use
the DSSM general framework to organize such a speech. Thus, the DSSM is
intended to promote flexible extemporaneous speaking skills without confining
the student within a rigid manuscript delivery.

The instructor should make it clear when assigning the speech that students
need to develop their ideas according to these ten steps. Thus, students have the
freedom to apply their own ideas within the basic framework. The outline can be
used as a basis for questions and answers and clarification regarding the
assignment. Students can readily conceptualize what is expected of them and
the initial steps of speech preparation.

The following Speech to Inform evaluation criteria are used for evaluation.
The evaluation criteria are numbered to correspond with the Speech to Inform

outline instructions. The reader can easily appreciate the rationale of the evaluation approach by comparing it against the speech outline instructions.

SPEECH TO INFORM EVALUATION SHEET

Name _____

Time _____

Grade _____

INTRODUCTION
  I. Opening
  II. Objective of speech
  III. Overview

BODY
  IV. Clarify importance of topic
  V. Main Idea: Inform the audience about your topic
  VI. Statement of sources
  VII. Sources the audience can refer to

CONCLUSION
  VIII. Review
  IX. Restatement of objective
  X. Closing

DELIVERY AND ADAPTATION TO AUDIENCE

VERBAL/NONVERBAL FACTORS

The evaluation outline should be given to students when the assignment is explained. This reiterates that evaluation of their speech will be based on their coverage of these ten steps. The length of the speech is also emphasized at the beginning of the evaluation. The evaluation process is clearly based on the DSSM Speech to Inform directives. This clarification helps relieve students' anxiety regarding what they need to do to meet the assigned objectives.

When students present their speeches, they are able to put more emphasis on delivery than would normally be the case if they did not have a concise outline. Delivery is enhanced because reduced anxiety means less tension and fewer mistakes. Anxiety reduction does much to make public speaking not only a learnable skill, but an enjoyable experience.

The Speech to Persuade/Actuate is a more complex process, but it can still be taught using the DSSM. The following provides a Speech to Persuade/Actuate outline using the DSSM. As with the Speech to Inform, the main idea is to stress the DSSM as a means of coherent speech organization without inhibiting creativity. Thus, the reader will see parallels between the Speech to Inform and the Speech to Persuade/Actuate.

INTRODUCTION
  I. OPENING ("Good afternoon. My name is . . .")
 II. OBJECTIVE OF SPEECH ("The objective of my speech to actuate is to persuade you to . . .")
III. OVERVIEW ("The main points I will cover in my speech to actuate are . . .")

BODY
 IV. STATEMENT OF PROBLEM (What is the problem that you are trying to persuade the audience to overcome? Why should the audience be interested in your topic?)
  V. STATEMENT OF SOLUTION (What is the solution to the problem that you are trying to persuade the audience to adopt?)
 VI. STATEMENT OF RATIONALE (Why is the intended solution the most logical answer to the problem?)
VII. STATEMENT OF IMPLEMENTATION (How can the intended solution be put into effect? What action does the audience need to take?)

CONCLUSION
VIII. REVIEW ("The main points I have covered in my speech to actuate are . . .")
 IX. RESTATEMENT OF OBJECTIVE ("The objective of my speech to actuate has been to persuade you to...")
  X. CLOSING

This speech outline is more complex than the Speech to Inform outline. Steps I through III and VIII through X are the same, but the body (steps IV through VII) is significantly different. The body of this speech is more closely intertwined than is the body of the Speech to Inform outline. The instructor should explain how the outlines differ when discussing the assignment in class.

Specifically, the instructor should emphasize the sequential progression of steps IV through VII of the Speech to Persuade/Actuate outline. This progression manifests a distinct building process whereby the speaker states the problem, solution, rationale for the solution, and how the solution can be implemented. Steps IV through VII of the Speech to Inform outline offer a building process, but the steps (and the ordering of the steps) are not as sophisticated as with the Speech to Persuade/Actuate outline. For instance, the order of the Speech to Inform outline steps (IV-VII) could be rearranged without detracting from the overall effect of DSSM usage.

The Speech to Inform helps students become comfortable with the DSSM and familiar with speaking from a key-word outline. A key-word outline is an outline that lists primary ideas of the speech but does not develop the ideas in full manuscript form. The Speech to Persuade/Actuate outline encourages students to use more sophisticated reasoning as they develop ideas to support their speech objectives. Again, the Speech to Persuade/Actuate outline is used as a base for questions and answers and clarification regarding the assignment. This helps students conceptualize what is expected of them and what their planning should involve.

Following are the Speech to Persuade/Actuate evaluation criteria.

SPEECH TO PERSUADE/ACTUATE EVALUATION SHEET
Name_____
Time_____
Grade_____

INTRODUCTION
I. Opening
II. Objective of speech
III. Overview

BODY
IV. Statement of problem
V. Statement of solution
VI. Statement of rationale
VII. Statement of implementation

CONCLUSION
VIII. Review
IX. Restatement of objective
X. Closing

DELIVERY AND ADAPTATION TO AUDIENCE

VERBAL/NONVERBAL FACTORS

ABILITY TO PERSUADE TO ACTION

As with the Speech to Inform, the instructor should give this evaluation outline to students when explaining the assignment. This approach underscores the importance of the ten steps. The length of the speech, delivery, adaptation, and overall ability to persuade to action are also emphasized in the evaluation. The evaluation process is clearly based on the DSSM Speech to Persuade/Actuate directives. Again, the reduction of anxiety regarding speech objectives results in less tension. Less tension generally results in more effective delivery and a positive response from the audience. Thus, a very useful skill (public speaking) has been learned or improved.

The Chinese educational system does not emphasize creativity and independent thinking nearly as much as the American educational system. Independent thinking is not compatible with Chinese socialist ideology. Chinese history is full of examples where independent thinkers have been persecuted. For instance, in the late 1950s Chairman Mao Tse Tung promoted the "Let a 100 flowers bloom" campaign (encouraging Chinese to freely express their views about Chinese society). After independent criticisms were freely stated, he proclaimed "We have enticed the snakes out of their holes" and severely persecuted those who had shared their criticisms. There are many examples of such persecution that ultimately encourage Chinese students (and citizens) to conform to prescribed government ideology.

Usage of the DSSM could have been ineffective in China because of the lack of creativity and independent thinking. However, the written survey, which is included in this paper, helped me bridge the instructional gap between the Chinese and American educational systems.

Although lacking, creativity is receiving more emphasis in the Chinese educational system as China continues to modernize and reform. "Since China is trying to modernize, the call for a new generation with both knowledge and originality is urgent" ("Originality Vital . . .," 1987). Teachers in China "no longer press their pupils to do mechanical memorization. . . . They tell children how to use their own minds. . . ." (Xing, 1987).

Before explaining the speech assignment, I surveyed student opinions and knowledge on public speaking issues to get a better understanding of their perspectives regarding speech preparation and delivery. The class surveyed was a freshman English class at Northern Jiaotong University in Beijing. Twenty-one students participated in the survey. The following is a summary of student responses to the survey. SA – strongly agree   A – agree   N – neutral   D –

disagree SD – strongly disagree

1. I feel my ability to speak English in front of a group of people is equal to my ability to understand English as a member of an audience.

SA	A	N	D	SD
10%	37%	19%	29%	5%

2. I am more nervous speaking English to a group of people than if I'm speaking English with one other person.

SA	A	N	D	SD
—	57%	10%	33%	—

3. I have received instructions on how to prepare and deliver a speech in English.

SA	A	N	D	SD
10%	29%	19%	32%	10%

4. I have received instruction on how to prepare and deliver a speech.

SA	A	N	D	SD
5%	47%	19%	19%	10%

5. I know how to prepare a (formal) outline for a speech.

SA	A	N	D	SD
—	72%	14%	14%	—

6. The purpose of a speech to inform is to persuade an audience to share your point of view and take some sort of action.

SA	A	N	D	SD
19%	47%	24%	10%	—

For the purpose of this chapter, questions four, five, and six are the most relevant.

Question four asked if they had received instruction on the preparation and delivery of a speech. Fifty-two percent indicated they had, and 29% indicated they had not (19% neutral).

Question five asked if they knew how to prepare a (formal) outline for a speech. Seventy-two percent indicated they could, and 14% indicated they could not (14% neutral).

Question six asked if the purpose of the speech to inform was to persuade an audience to share one's point of view and take some sort of action. Sixty-six percent of the students agreed with this statement, and only ten percent disagreed (24% neutral). Question six posed a blatantly incorrect statement, which only ten percent of the students answered correctly. The question was asked to measure their understanding of common American approaches to public speaking.

Based on information gathered during the survey and my overall impression of students' English speaking ability, I used the DSSM in a manner similar to applications in the U.S. The primary difference involved more lengthy explanations for each step of the process and what students needed to do to meet the speech objectives. This approach provided direction for effective speechmaking and helped students develop their application of original ideas. This finding is based on the quality of speeches given in class.

The Developmental Speech Sequence Model, as a teaching alternative, represents an approach that can have positive ramifications in other areas of instruction. Any types of self expression and organization, such as speaking and writing, draw upon students' abilities to organize their thoughts and present their ideas in a coherent manner. Directions for such objectives can be detailed, whether they be for speaking or writing, but not necessarily at the expense of creativity. The goal of this model is to emphasize creativity within the common ground of detailed instruction.

References

Ahrendt, K.M. (ed.) *Teaching the Developmental Education Student.* San Francisco: Jossey-Bass, 1987.

Boylan, H.R. *Is Developmental Education Working? An Analysis of Research.* A research report prepared for the National Association for Developmental Education (Spring 1983).

Cross, P.D. *Accent on Learning.* San Francisco: Jossey-Bass, 1976.

Lehr, J.B., and H.W. Harris. *At-Risk, Low-Achieving Students in the Classroom.* Washington, D.C.: National Education Association, 1988.

"Originality Vital to Students," *China Daily* (June 6, 1987), p. 4.

Roueche J.E., and G.A. Baker. *Access and Excellence: The Open-Door College.* Washington, D.C.: The Community College Press, 1987.

Roueche, J.E., and J.J. Snow. *Overcoming Learning Problems.* San Francisco: Jossey-Bass, 1977.

Roueche, J.E., and C.L. Wheeler. "Instructional Procedures for the Disadvantaged," *Improving College and University Teaching,* Summer 1973.

Shapiro, E.S. *Academic Skills Problems: Direct Assessment and Intervention.* New York: Guilford Press, 1989.

Xing, L. "Teachers Try to Make Chinese Easier to Learn," *China Daily* (June 10, 1987), p. 4.
Zehr, E.S. *Reading, Writing: A Tutorial Guide in the Language Arts.* Blacksburg, Virginia: Rowan Mountain Press, 1990.

Chapter Thirteen

International Media Events as Instructional Tools in the Basic Communication Course

Since the People's Republic of China opened to the outside world in 1979, it has engaged in a variety of reforms to help it compete economically on the world market. A key problem for the government has centered on how to adopt economic reforms without adopting corresponding political reforms. Seeds of student unrest, regarding the lack of political reforms, were evidenced during student protests in the winter of 1987. The protests were silenced, but discontent with the small-scale political reforms persisted. Meanwhile, significant economic reforms continued.

In spring 1989 students mounted another protest in Tiananmen Square (the public square in the capital city of Beijing), seeking democratic political reforms. Roughly 3,000 students engaged in a hunger strike that quickly gathered support from various segments of the Chinese population. Tiananmen Square is the largest plaza in the world (roughly 100 acres) and at times during the protest held over one million people. Western media, in Beijing to report on the Gorbachev visit (and the significant Chinese-Soviet summit indicating normalization between the two communist superpowers), had a rare opportunity to cover the massive protest in China. The Gorbachev visit was quickly dwarfed as the uprising gained momentum throughout the country.

On June 3 the protest came to a bloody end when Chinese troops killed an estimated 3,000 Chinese citizens in and around Tiananmen Square. The military action received considerable condemnation worldwide. The following days saw random firing on Chinese citizens and foreigners in Beijing and overt intimidation of the Chinese population. The uprising, and especially the crackdown, are seen as major setbacks for China.

This chapter will emphasize use of international media events, such as the uprising in China, as an instructional tool in the basic communication course. Actual film footage, produced by western journalists reporting from China, can be used for case study analysis of perception concepts exemplified in the events reported. Perceptual processes can be recognized in the events and the reporting of events. The latter is especially fruitful for analysis. Regarding the Chinese protests, NBC News anchor Tom Brokaw stated, "I think a big part of what people are looking for is context and perspective" (Collins and Donlon, 1989, p. 3D).

According to Devito (1989, pp. 38-41), perception is divided into three stages: 1) sensory stimulation occurs, 2) sensory stimulations are organized, and 3) sensory stimulations are interpreted and evaluated. Attribution, the process used to understand behaviors of others and attribute motivations for these behaviors, occurs in the third stage. Causality, internal and external, is a factor in this attribution process. American reporters, academic experts, and government representatives were caught off guard when the protests quickly escalated. They could barely report the events, let alone speculate what might happen in the future. In this reporting of events much emphasis was given on *what* was happening and *why* it was happening. Thus, attribution for the behaviors reported became a primary element in news stories broadcast from China.

This particular case study examines the May 18, 1989, CBS News documentary *48 Hours*. Analysis deals with the frustrations felt by western journalists as they worked to understand the series of events in China. Their confusion was conveyed directly and, at times, indirectly. A key objective for journalists was to convey the perceptual context of Chinese citizens so that it was understandable to the U.S. perceptual context. News reports were frequently prefaced and concluded with disclaimers regarding the accuracy of their sources. Speculation was essential throughout the reporting. Thus, the role of perception was clearly evidenced and is suitable for analysis in the classroom.

The *48 Hours* episode was entitled "China Rebellion." It was a live broadcast from Beijing, China, and offered an excellent opportunity to watch the CBS News team present news with little preparation. The student protest had just spread to many other areas of the Chinese society, and the ramifications of the events were major for China. "China Rebellion" featured six primary segments focusing on: 1) the hunger strike in Beijing, 2) individual hunger strikers, 3) a political analysis and the goal of free speech, 4) hunger strikers in Shanghai, 5) Chinese students in the U.S. and an analysis by a China expert, and 6) a closing commentary by Charles Kuralt (a CBS journalist). A videotape copy of the "China Rebellion" episode can be obtained by writing "48 Hours," CBS News, CBS Inc., 51 W. 52nd St., New York, NY 10019.

I use the case study approach in the basic course to enhance student learning of theory and application of theory. That is, I describe theoretical concepts and emphasize student ability to apply or recognize the concepts in various contexts. In this particular case study, perception theory is used. The following steps detail use of the *48 Hours* "China Rebellion" episode.

1) Perception theory is discussed in class. The stages of perception,

attribution theory and the role of causality (internal and external) are stressed.

2) Students are assured that they do not need to know anything about China to do well in their analysis. Observance of the *48 Hours* episode will be sufficient.

3) Discussion of broadcast journalist objectives to report who, what, when, where, why, and how. This case study emphasizes the "what" secondarily and the "why" primarily.

4) Description of how CBS News journalists were in China to report on the Chinese-Soviet summit, the student protests occurred unexpectedly, many segments of the Chinese population joined in the uprising, and the uprising became far more important than the Chinese-Soviet summit. Journalists worked to report and interpret events as they occurred.

5) Considerable cross-cultural interpretation was needed due to the differences between Chinese and American societies. For instance, China is communist controlled and uses a socialist economic system. The U.S. is governed through democracy and uses a capitalist economic system.

6) Cross-cultural interpretation requires emphasis on the perceptual bases of the compared cultures. Thus, the "why" aspect of reported events needs clarification.

7) Students observe the *48 Hours* "China Rebellion" videotape and are instructed to answer three questions. 1) How do journalists explain what is happening? 2) How do journalists explain why it is happening? and 3) Are the protests a result of internal or external causality? Why? Their responses are presented in a 1 to 2 page reaction paper.

This type of case study approach can be used with a variety of theoretical concepts and international media events. I chose this particular event because I was a visiting professor in Beijing, China, in 1987 and my familiarity with China's modernization enhances my ability to understand responses on the subject. Use of the assignment has been beneficial and, in addition to the emphasis on perception, provides examples for reference during lectures on other topics.

Similar applications, with other theoretical concepts and international media events, can also be used for case study analysis. Analysis of group think, as it existed in the Kennedy administration during the Bay of Pigs invasion (in Cuba), can be emphasized with news footage from that time period. Cross-cultural high context gestures, as they exist between the U.S. and Iraq, can also be studied in nightly network news broadcasts. The CBS news address previously listed can be a helpful source for obtaining copies of such news broadcasts.

Use of international media events as an instructional tool in the basic course is an excellent way to integrate world events into the curriculum. As international trade and exchange continue to grow, it is increasingly important for students to be aware of other cultures and how they contrast with the U.S. on the interpersonal, organizational, and societal levels. This type of assignment enhances such awareness.

References

Collins, M., and Donlon, B. *USA Today.* June 6, 1989, p. 3D.
Devito, J.A. *The Interpersonal Communication Book.* New York: Harper & Row, 1989.

Section Three

HEALTH

Chapter Fourteen

The Merging of Traditional Chinese Medicine and Western Medicine in China

The People's Republic of China is engaged in reforms which involve development of its economic, cultural, educational, and political processes. The need for reform has been realized, as China has fallen behind the development of the western world in many areas. China closed its doors to the outside world in 1949, and it experienced limited interaction with the outside world until reform began in 1979.

The cultural revolution (1966-1976) was especially hard on development in China. During this period, political upheaval discouraged, and in some cases banned, technological developments. Since 1979, though, China has focused considerable emphasis on developing itself and promoting more interaction with the western world.

One of the many areas which has received modernization efforts is medicine. The medical treatment in China is based on the practices of Traditional Chinese Medicine (TCM). Traditional Chinese Medicine has evolved during China's long history, which dates back over 5,000 years.

The effectiveness of TCM has not been questioned, but Chinese physicians have sought to better understand TCM by seeking interaction with western physicians. The intended result is that both Chinese and western medical practices can be enhanced through cross-cultural collaboration.

In September 1981, the *Journal of Traditional Chinese Medicine* was founded by the All-China Association of Traditional Chinese Medicine and the Academy of Traditional Chinese Medicine. The journal was the first English periodical of Traditional Chinese Medicine published in China.

In the first issue Chui Yueli, President of the All-China Association of Traditional Chinese Medicine, states, "Traditional Chinese Medicine is not a treasure belonging to the Chinese people alone, but it is an integral part of world civilization and a common benefit for all mankind. . . . All Chinese-Western collaboration has shown more satisfactory results than could have been expected with either western or traditional Chinese medicine alone" (Yueli, 1981, p. v).

Traditional Chinese Medicine has proven to be effective within the Chinese culture, and some practices have been exported to western nations. One such example is acupuncture. Although Chinese practitioners are confident in their methods, and they have little problem explaining "how" the procedures are to be performed, they have expressed difficulty explaining "why" the procedures are effective.

Interaction with western physicians provides a climate whereby western physicians can learn more about "how" and "why" the procedures are effective. Thus, through the merging of TCM and western medicine, old ideas are being cross-culturally communicated through new perspectives. This chapter will discuss how considerations affecting the merging have evolved since the open-door reforms were initiated by the People's Republic of China in 1979.

Interaction between Chinese physicians and western physicians has increased significantly since the opening of China. Dr. Kie Zhufan, head of Traditional Chinese Medicine at Beijing Medical College, lectured and did research on the integration of TCM and western medical systems during a six month period in 1981 ("Dr. Kie Zhufan Invited...," 1981, p. 97). This is recognized as one of the seeds of the many exchanges which have occurred since.

A symposium sponsored by France's International Health Centre, held in April 1987, exemplifies the many medical exchanges which have occurred during the 1980s. A Chinese delegation met with government officials from ten western European nations during the three day symposium. "They had an indepth exchange of views on western and Chinese traditional medicine, their different viewpoints and methods, and their past development and present state. They also explored fresh channels for greater cooperation in the field" ("East-West Work," 1987).

Traditional Chinese Medicine is a legacy composed of centuries of experiences by the Chinese in dealing with disease. These experiences have evolved into a unique system of theories and beliefs. A discussion of medical exchange between China and the west must consider fundamental ideas of TCM, which are foreign to western medicine. The Yin and Yang and the five elements exemplify such ideas.

Yin and Yang holds that everything in the universe is composed of two opposite aspects which are constantly interdependent and in conflict. Water and fire symbolize basic properties of Yin and Yang. "That is to say, the basic properties of Yin stimulate those of water, including coldness, downward direction, dimness, etc., while the basic properties of Yang are like those of fire, including heat, upward direction, brightness, etc." ("Lectures on Essentials...," 1981, p. 73).

The theory of the five elements maintains that wood, fire, earth, metal and water are the basic materials which comprise the physical world. A relationship of interdependence and interrestraint exists among these elements. A fundamental premise of Traditional Chinese Medicine is to "classify natural phenomena, tissues and organs of the human body and human emotions, into different categories and to interpret the relationship between human physiology and pathology and the natural environment with the law of the interpromoting, interacting, overacting, and counteracting of the five elements" ("Lectures on Essentials...," 1981, p. 77). This premise is central to their medical practice.

The merging of TCM with western medicine has been done effectively in a variety of areas.

> They have used combined Chinese and western medical means to treat acute abdomens, bone fracture, arthritis, soft tissue trauma, coronary heart disease. ... All have shown more satisfactory results than could have been expected with either western or traditional Chinese medicine alone. At the same time a deeper insight has been gained into the nature of certain diseases and the mechanisms for recovery. (Yueli, 1981, p. v)

The practice of acupuncture, the 3,000 year old Chinese practice of using needles to treat a wide range of illnesses, by western physicians has received much attention in the past decade. Acupuncture is now taught in the west. The Hwa To Acupuncture Centre, in the Netherlands, was the first school in the west to grant full Chinese diplomas for acupuncture study. "The object of the whole exercise is to come to a synthesis of western medicine and traditional Chinese medicine in the hope it benefits patients" says Henk Termeulen, director of the Centre ("Chance Meeting Spawns...," 1987).

The combining of Traditional Chinese Medicine and western medicine has also been used for patients with orthopedic problems. Wang Congshu, president of Baoding Orthopedics Rehabilitation Hospital, cures orthopedic illnesses "by using qigong, or Chinese traditional breathing exercises, combined with other Chinese traditional and western methods" ("Old and New Combine...," 1987). Benefits of combining approaches have also been realized in the radiation treatment of cancer ("China Leads in...," 1987) and the removal of gallstones ("Shock Waves Remove...," 1987).

Concern with the connection between mental well being and physical well being has received increased emphasis in the U.S. in the past 20 years. A similar emphasis has occurred in China. The Sino-Japan Friendship Hospital, founded in 1984, bases its approaches on western and TCM. Cheng Lirong, a nurse at the hospital, reports, "One characteristic of nursing is emotion nursing, similar to psychological nursing in the west" (Jianhua, 1987). It is believed that seven emotional factors (joy, anger, melancholy, brooding, sorrow, fear, and shock) can cause disease.

The merging of TCM with western medicine has produced many benefits, but there have been problems which have hindered the process. "Differences in historical backgrounds and language barriers still place some limits on international academic exchange concerning traditional Chinese medicine and integrated Chinese and western medicine. This is particularly so in the west, where many medical workers are unfamiliar with traditional Chinese medicine" (Yueli, 1981, p. v).

Cultural norms have also hindered the exchange of medical practices. Blood transfusions have become more common in China "but it is still difficult to find enough donors because of a traditional Chinese fear of losing blood," reports Xing Lixiang, a senior official of the Beijing Blood Centre (Tingting, 1987).

Yu Fangouing, director of the maternity ward at Beijing Hospital for Gynecology and Obstetrics, points out that many women are reluctant to use new practices based on scientific approaches. "They stick to their old-fashioned teachings of their mothers or in-laws and make a list of taboos after delivery— abstaining from taking a bath, cleaning their teeth, eating fruits and getting out of bed within one month of delivery. Babies are completely bound up for one month" (Manhong, 1987).

Another consideration which directly contrasts with practices in the west deals with wages for physicians and health care staff. Chinese physicians and health care staff make far less money than western physicians and staff. "A doctor in Beijing's Chaoyang Hospital has to see up to 60 patients a day, but gets a monthly wage of less than 80 yuan ($21 U.S.)" (Guanfeng, 1987). This amount is less than the wage of teachers in China, which is another low paying occupation. Thus, one can safely assume that the health care field in China is valued differently than it is in the United States (where medical doctors make much more money proportionate to their counterparts in China).

The merging of TCM with western medicine in China exemplifies a situation where old ideas are cross-culturally communicated through new perspectives. That is, Chinese medical approaches are explained through western perspectives. Though there are hinderances within this process, the benefits have been viewed as being well worth the costs (obstacles which have been encountered). This chapter has described the benefits of such interaction, and some of the problems which have arisen, in hopes of better understanding a process which can continue to improve health care practices around the world.

References

"Chance Meeting Spawns Acupuncture Centre," *China Daily* (April 22, 1987), p. 1.

"China Leads in Cancer Treatment," *China Daily* (April 28, 1987), p. 3.

"Dr. Kie Zhufan Invited to Lecture in USA," *Journal of Traditional Chinese Medicine* (Vol. 1, No. 2) December 1981, p. 97.

"East-West Work Urged in Medicine," *China Daily* (April 6, 1987), p. 4.

Guanfeng, C. "Top Expert Warns of Shortage of Doctors," *China Daily* (March 31, 1987), p. 1.

Jianhua, A. "Nurse Tailors Her Care," *China Daily* (April 6, 1987), p. 6.

"Lectures on Essentials of Traditional Chinese Medicine," *Journal of Traditional Chinese Medicine* (Vol. 1, No. 1) September 1981, p. 73.

Manhong, S. "Teaching Science of Nurture," *China Daily* (April 16, 1987), p. 5.

Meizhong, Y. "To My Colleagues," *Journal of Traditional Chinese Medicine* (Vol. 1, No. 1) September, 1981, p. i.

"Old and New Combine to Heal," *China Daily* (May 14, 1987), p. 6.

"Shock Waves Remove Gallstones," *China Daily* (April 8, 1987), p. 5.

Tingting, Z. "Blood Donors Get New Incentives," *China Daily* (April 20, 1987), p. 3.

Yueli, C. "A Welcome Event in International Academic Exchange on Traditional Chinese Medicine," *Journal of Traditional Chinese Medicine* (Vol. 1, No. 1) September, 1981, p. v.

Chapter Fifteen

A Cross-Cultural Interpretation of China's One-Child-Per-Family Campaign Using Burke's Rhetoric of Transcendence

Coauthored with Pei Wang (first author)

Kenneth Burke's rhetoric of transcendence offers a beneficial framework for interpreting mass communication campaigns. This chapter uses the rhetoric of transcendence to cross-culturally interpret the one-child-per-family campaign in the People's Republic of China. Data for the study were collected through reviews of literature and firsthand accounts in China. Pei Wang, the first author, was raised in Beijing, received undergraduate training in south China, and served as a foreign affairs officer in Beijing before coming to the U.S.

Overpopulation is a major problem for developing countries such as the People's Republic of China (the Chinese population has doubled in the past 30 years). After the ten year "cultural revolution" (1966-1976) the Chinese government was stunned to find how fast its population had increased. Despite family planning that encouraged couples to raise two to three children, a demographic analysis in 1978 indicated that the population would reach 1.3 billion after 20 years and 1.5 billion after 40 years with the existing birth rate of 2.3 children per couple. This implied that no matter how hard people worked to improve their living conditions, a considerable amount of financial and material resources would have to be used for feeding, clothing and housing the growing population.

China actively initiated a modernization campaign in 1979 by emphasizing four modernizations (agriculture, industry, science and technology, and national defense). Overpopulation was recognized as an obstacle to China's modernization. As a result, in 1979 the Chinese government announced that the country should reduce its population growth rate to 0.5% by 1985 and zero by the turn of the century in order to achieve its modernization objectives. This meant that each couple could have only one child. This practice would have to last for at least 20 years.

Even with people understanding the importance of population control, enforcement of the one-child-per-family practice was recognized as a major task by the Chinese government. Thus, the government launched a one-child-per-family campaign in 1979. "The flourishing of science has been so vigorous that we have not yet had time to make a spiritual readjustment adequate to the changes in our resources of material and knowledge" (Burke, 1964, p. 22).

Family planning became a state policy and was written into the country's constitution. Former Premier Zhao Ziyang acknowledged that family planning would not be possible simply through economic sanctions and coercion ("Premier Zhao Ziyang Explains . . .," 1987). Stewart et al. (1984) state that "no regime can long survive on a threat of force alone. Communication is the most important means of social order, for within communication lies the power to create and control images that legitimate authority" (p. 27). Rogers (1973) points out that "a campaign is a pre-planned set of communication activities designed by change agents to achieve certain change in receiver behavior in a specified time period" (p. 78). This is exactly what the Chinese government has tried to accomplish in the campaign.

According to Kenneth Burke, human beings are symbol-creating, symbol-using, and symbol-misusing animals (Burke, 1989, p. 62). Symbols form the basis of people's overt behavior. Therefore, human action is the by-product or the stimulus of symbols. "The 'transcendence' of man's symbol systems operates in many ways, even when the terminology is supposedly designed for quite different purposes" (Burke, 1961, p. 38). Since people cooperate with each other through symbolic interactions, persuasion is inherent in the nature of symbolism. Persuasion and communication are interrelated (Stewart et al. 1984, p. 33). "Persuasion involves choice, will; it is directed to a man only insofar as he is free" (Burke, 1969, p. 50).

Since the one-child family campaign is a nationwide campaign, the government has employed every possible medium to communicate the policy. The purpose of the campaign is to persuade people to practice family planning so that the population can be reduced. By examining the symbolic actions taken by the government during the past 20 years, an understanding of the campaign's effectiveness can be gauged. "When we use symbols for things, such symbols are not merely reflections of the things symbolized, or signs for them; they are to a degree a transcending of the things symbolized" (Burke, 1989, p. 200).

Kenneth Burke's well known "rhetoric of transcendence" is useful for analysis of campaign persuasive strategies. Burke sees transcendence as a "static" way for people to lift themselves above their problems (Burke, 1989, p. 202). In a rhetoric of transcendence, persuaders argue that a person, thing, goal, purpose, or an action is superior to others of its kind. The key categories of comparison are quantity (more-less), quality (good-bad), value (important-unimportant), and hierarchy (high-low). The strategy of transcendence provides persuaders with scales for arguments. "When approached from a certain point of view, A and B are 'opposites.' We mean by 'transcendence' the adoption of another point of view from which they cease to be opposites" (Burke, 1989, p. 275).

Burke's rhetoric of transcendence emphasizes essence. This emphasis is exemplified in the relationship between the individual words of a sentence and their total meaning. For example, "the syllables of the words are 'born' and 'die.' But the meaning of those syllables 'transcends' their sheer nature as temporal motions. It is an essence, not reducible to any part of the sentence, or even to the whole of it" (Burke, 1961, p. 142).

The one-child family campaign uses various communication channels for advocating the policy. To urge people to practice family planning, the government has not only employed mass media to explain why the country needs such a policy, but it also uses interpersonal channels to inform citizens about birth control. These two complementary channels serve the same purpose in different ways.

Mass media is a pervasive form of communication. Therefore, the government tries to make full use of all forms of mass media to convey the campaign message to the people. Newspapers, magazines, television, radio, governmental documents, novels, films, plays, songs, slogans, billboards and posters have all been used as sources for advocating the policy throughout the campaign. The policy obviously calls on Chinese citizens to make a very unique sacrifice. The necessity of this sacrifice, as emphasized by the government, is the foundation of the campaign. Burke (1972) maintains that "the sacrificial principle itself is integral to the social order" (p. 38). The following describes how various mass media forms are used to promote the campaign.

The *People's Daily* is the most widely distributed newspaper in China. It periodically has a front page editorial describing how the one-child-per-family campaign contributes to a better quality of life in China. This type of editorial does not present new information, but it does serve as message reinforcement.

The Chinese government produces a magazine called *Marriage and Family Planning* that promotes the one-child policy. Poems, such as "Mother Earth," are frequently featured in such magazines. "Mother Earth" explains that the earth provides life like a mother but has limited resources that we all need to strive to conserve. Limiting population growth helps conserve resources.

C.C.T.V. (China Central T.V.) is used to promote the policy. Benefits and updates regarding the policy are mentioned on the news, themes supporting the one-child message are found in T.V. dramas, and "The Best Child Contest" (described later in this article) is broadcast on television, which is becoming more common throughout China.

Radio stations frequently carry public service announcements describing the percentage of the Chinese population that has pledged to be a one-child family and how these families receive special privileges. They report strategies used by work units to encourage members to make such a pledge. Songs with campaign themes are also played. Two primary target groups are grandparents and farmers, because these two populations tend to be least supportive of the policy.

Government documents are circulated on how the population control objective is being addressed. Such documents, that describe what's been achieved and what the future goals are, are generally distributed via work units. Family planning is also a regular segment of the country's annual report (much like the State of the Union address in the U.S.).

A Late Awakening is a typical novel that has a one-child theme. This novel is directed at farmers. It deals with a farm wife who realizes too late in life that having more than one child leads to a lower quality of life. This perspective needs frequent emphasis because it contradicts traditional Chinese beliefs.

Similarly, a film entitled "Women Are Human Beings Too" portrays the plight of a woman who is being coerced by her mother-in-law into having a child. The mother-in-law yearns for a grandson. The daughter-in-law has heart disease and is warned by her doctor that a pregnancy could be fatal. The woman becomes pregnant, at her mother-in-law's insistence, and she dies during pregnancy.

"A Family's Self-Inflicted Burden" is a popular play about a family that has two children (both girls) and is trying to give birth to a boy. They move from town to town since they have stigmatized themselves by violating the one-child policy. Their family has little stability and the parents must work menial labor to make ends meet. Their drive to have a son, and the consequent violation of the one-child policy, cause minimal quality of life. Thus, even if they do have a son, the happiness of having a son will be over-shadowed by not being able to provide adequately for him or the rest of the family.

Songs in support of the campaign have been written to portray various perspectives (i.e., children's, parent's, and grandparent's). "We Should Never Forget Family Planning" proclaims:

> Family planning is the fundamental government policy. Have fewer kids later, they'll be more healthy. The country will prosper this way...leading to a better life. In order to achieve this quality of life each couple should have only one child. Family planning should never be forgotten.

"Ten Reasons for a Family Planning Bill" outlines ten reasons in support of the one-child policy. The refrain of this song states, "Family planning needs to be a bill to enable more thorough enforcement of the one-child policy." These types of songs substantiate the need for family planning.

Chinese society emphasizes slogans more often than what is practiced in the U.S. The slogans can be seen on billboards, banners, and work unit blackboards. Chinese slogans do not necessarily rhyme but generally they do have an equal number of characters per line. The following examples are typical family planning slogans.

1) "We should reduce our population by the year 2000." 2) "It is good to practice family planning." 3) "Practice family planning, control the population, improve quality of life...these are fundamental and national policies." 4) "For the future of the nation and the happiness of future generations, practice family planning (have fewer but better children)." 5) "Laws are needed to control over-population."

Billboards in the U.S. usually advertise a product. Billboards in China are more often public service announcements. One can frequently see, at major street intersections, billboards depicting a happy Chinese family (father, mother, and one child). The one child is usually a girl. This is intended to counter the general societal preference for a boy.

Posters are mass produced for posting in work units. These posters usually convey public service type concerns (such as safety). One such topic commonly stresses the one-child policy. For example, calendars are produced that have each month emphasizing a different public service concern. Family planning is one such concern.

In 1980, the Central Committee of the Chinese Communist Party issued an "open letter" urging couples to stop childbearing after one child. The letter states, "The State Council has called for the practice of one-child-per-couple. The program is an important measure which concerns the speed and future of the realization of the four modernizations and the health and happiness of future generations. This measure conforms to the immediate and longer-term interests of all people" ("Open Letter," 1980). In 1982, the 12th Communist Party Congress and the Fifth National Peoples Congress announced that family planning must be understood as an implementation of state law and the party discipline. Article 25 of the Constitution of the People's Republic of China stipulates that the state promotes family planning so that population growth may fit the plan for economic and social development. In 1987, at the Second Asian Population and Development Forum held in Beijing, former Chinese Premier Zhao Ziyang said in his opening speech that China has made population control a state policy. "It is not only for the prosperity and happiness of the Chinese people, but it also benefits the whole world in terms of population stabilization and economic development" (Zhao, *Report of the Second . . .,* 1987).

It should be pointed out that, although family planning has been written into China's constitution, the one-child-per-family policy is not a constitutional law. Rather, the need for one-child-per-family adherence is strongly stated. The government explains that population growth has to match society's ability to care for the population. Thus, one-child-per-family is seen as a temporary policy, until the population stabilizes at a lower (more manageable) number.

China is divided into provinces (similar to state divisions in the U.S.). Each province makes its own rule regarding enforcement of "effective family planning." The overall approach within provinces is to reward adherence first and punish violations as a last resort.

Couples that sign pledges to have only one child receive special privileges such as time off from work and benefits for their one child (i.e., health care and education). In general terms, the family is viewed favorably by the government. If they give birth to a retarded child they may have a second child.

Each couple gets only one "residency card" (similar to a birth certificate). This residency card provides the basic needs for that child. A second child is not eligible for these basic services (food, housing, health care, education, etc.). The government does not provide birthing help with the child. Basically, the second child is a non-person.

Fining can occur to penalize parents for the cost of the child to society, even though the child receives no formal privileges. The Communist Party may blatantly embarrass violators as a lesson to other couples.

The rhetorical strategies used by the Chinese government exemplify rhetorical transcendence. Kenneth Burke explains that transcendence is the "building of a terministic bridge whereby one realm is transcended by being viewed in terms of a realm beyond it" (Stewart et al. 1989, p. 176). According to Burke, one of the common methods of establishing transcendence stresses hierarchy. Arguments which are based on hierarchy attempt to establish that one thing, or act, exceeds another because it is of higher order along a graduation or continuum (Stewart et al. 1984, p. 87). This is a major line of argument the government uses to justify this policy.

Burke describes "two movements in a Platonist dialectic. First, there is the 'Upward Way' from 'lower terms' to a unitary transcendent term...then there is a reversal of direction, a 'Downward Way,' back to the 'lower' terms with which the dialectician began his climb" (Burke, 1961, p. 37). A continuum is implied in this conceptual framework.

We assume that how many children a couple should have is a private affair, and individuals should have their own right to make decisions in this area. The

Chinese government tells its people that this individual decision is directly related to the well-being of the present and future generations. What the argument implies is that the needs of the country are more important than those of individuals. Thus, according to the government, it is an honorary action to make a personal sacrifice by having only one child.

Burke's concept of rhetorical transcendence maintains that hierarchy is only one of the ways to achieve transcendence. The government does not rely on this one line of argument alone. The government has established arguments based on all common points of comparison (quality, quantity, and value) in addition to hierarchy. It is helpful to remember that "substitution sets the condition for 'transcendence,' since there is a technical sense in which the name for a thing can be said to 'transcend' the thing named (by making a kind of 'ascent' from the realm of motion and matter to the realm of essence and spirit)" (Burke, 1957, p. 62).

The argument the government provides in terms of comparison of quality is that the quality of the population can be improved by implementing the one-child-per-family policy. One of the most frequently seen slogans of the campaign is "Giving birth to and raising healthier babies and improving the quality of the population." The logic of this argument is that by having only one child the state and parents can afford to give better care to the children. Therefore, the children will be better off both physically and intellectually. Burke (1957) states that a "slogan is not widely effective because it rises spontaneously in every part of the country (it is usually one man's invention); a slogan is widely effective because it is appropriate to a widespread situation" (p. 72).

During the past 20 years, the government has given special considerations to the children in one-child families in terms of nursery care, medical treatment, school, and housing distribution. In order to demonstrate the benefits of having one child per couple, one of the many things the government has done is to hold "The Best Child Contest" each year. The candidates, who are all from single-child families, are judged in terms of their intellectual level and healthiness. The contest is televised live to the whole country.

The government uses examples and various art forms to show how life can be much different for children and parents in a family with many kids. One such example deals with Karl Marx, a well known socialist theorist. The story tells how he regretted having so many children for whom he could not adequately care. One of his children died of illness resulting from lack of good health care. In this case the government established a qualitative comparison between the well-off and the poor.

Another line of argument is established on the basis of comparison of quantity. During the campaign, the government has released statistical information showing the interrelationships among family size, production, natural resources, and living standards. The statistical information has provided people with concrete pictures of what kind of problems the country would run into if the population grew unchecked. Without population control, China's population would reach two billion by 2020. Such being the case, half of China's efforts to promote the state economy would have to be used to meet the basic needs of the surplus population. An article published in *China—Facts and Figures* states, "If the target of controlling population growth (keeping it within 1.2 billion by the turn of the century) is successfully met, the per capita gross value of industrial and agricultural production should increase from 719.6 yuan in 1980 to 2,333.3 yuan in 2000" ("Population," 1984). The *Zhongshan University Journal* compares family size and basic needs in the year 2000. The table indicates what will be the average amounts of farmland, food grain, number of children entering primary school, and total nurturing expenses incurred in relation to the average births of 3, 2.3, 2, 1.5 and 1 per couple, respectively. From these figures, people can easily see the logic for choosing the one-child family option (*Zhongshan University Journal*, 1984).

The last line of argument is comparison of value. This is aimed at combating feudalist influence. China is a country with more than 2000 years of feudalism. Therefore, many feudalist ideas are still deeply rooted in Chinese society. One example that reflects feudalist influence is that many people hold the belief that the male is respectable, while the female is lowly. Since one couple can have only one child, many people prefer a boy. Since the implementation of the policy, there have been numerous cases where parents abandoned or killed their girl infants in the hope that they could have another baby. Realizing that this is not a simple issue of preference, but of value, the government has made tremendous efforts to convince its people that men and women are equally valuable and capable. In this respect, literature and arts have played an active role in promoting equality of the sexes.

There is a popular Chinese movie called "The Sweet Career," which appeared in the 1980s. It tells a story about a family of five girls whose parents want to have a boy. In the end they get a son, a son-in-law. The eldest daughter's husband decides to move in with the family instead of following the social custom of bringing the wife to stay with his family. It is unrealistic to say that a movie can totally change value systems. However, little by little, people are changing. It is more common for a son-in-law to stay with the woman's family. It is not considered disgraceful or humiliating any more. The idea that women are as capable as men is gaining acceptance.

This chapter describes how various forms of mass media are used to advocate the one-child policy. The word "mass" indicates the audiences. Even   though the targets of family planning are younger generations, in the public propaganda, the government does not make any special references as to whom it makes the appeals. It gives people the impression that everybody is equally responsible for the implementation of the policy. This is an effective use of strategic ambiguity.   Population control cannot be achieved through the efforts of a single generation. It is also the responsibility of generations to come. In this sense, the propaganda tends to influence not only the present young parents but also future parents. Moreover, the family is a system, which means its members influence and are influenced by each other. By reaching the older generations, the government can win their support for the policy and use influence from older generations to affect the child-bearing age generation.

Even though mass media is a powerful and prevalent form of communication, it cannot guarantee that people will do what is desired. Attitude and behavior do not always have a direct cause and effect relationship. There can always exist a gap between attitude and behavior, or between knowledge and behavior. This is why the government introduced emphasis on interpersonal communication regarding family planning.

Not long after the one-child campaign was started, the state required that each work unit set up its own family planning supervision committee. What the committee does is supervise the implementation of the policy and provide personal and professional guidance on birth control. The committee members are very familiar with the people they are working with and are always ready to offer help when necessary. Their efforts are directed primarily toward young parents and newly married couples.

Before any couple can get their marriage certificate, they have to go to a designated hospital for a physical checkup and for lectures on birth control. After the lectures, everybody is given some written materials to keep. All the publications stress family planning and raising "fewer but healthier babies." Unlike mass media, the persuasion through interpersonal communication is more flexible in content and form. The members may borrow arguments from official sources. However, most of the time, they adapt to their specific audience and specific situation. The following paragraph describes an approach used by one committee member. "She [committee member/propagandist] held no formal meetings for her group but at each monthly production meeting she put family planning on the agenda for a report or discussion. She frequently spoke with the women individually. She distributed free contraceptives at least once a month and generally kept an eye on their health and their attitude towards the policy" (Fieldnotes, 1991). Free contraceptives are also distributed to men.

Interpersonal communication plays an important role in the one-child family campaign. It is through interpersonal communication that the gap between attitude and behavior is greatly minimized.

It's been twenty years since the campaign started. China has been able to keep the population within 1.3 billion by 2000. Following are ways to gauge the effectiveness of the campaign.

First, the arguments developed by the government are influential and effective. The emphasis on the relationship between population control and economic development is particularly relevant at this time. The Chinese people have fresh memories of the cultural revolution upheaval (1966-1976) and are anxious to improve their living standard. The 1989 pro-democracy movement exemplifies the interest in changing with the world. Therefore, the use of rhetorical transcendence, in which the goal of economic development is placed in a higher order than the goal of individual immediate happiness, works very well. People are just as eager to modernize the country as the government is, so they are ready to accept the one-child arguments and to respond to the government's appeals.

Second, the use of both mass media and interpersonal communication has proven to be effective. According to the *People's Daily*, the country's birth rate and natural growth rate decreased from 3.34% and 2.58% in the 1970s to 1.78% and 1.12%, respectively, in 1985 ("The Chinese Population . . .," 1987). As far as the short term objective is concerned, the campaign did not succeed in achieving the goal of reducing the natural growth rate to 0.5% by 1985. However, this does not suggest that the campaign is a failure. As a result of birth peaks in the mid-1950s and subsequently in the mid-1960s, it was expected that some 20 million persons would enter marriage and child bearing age annually between 1976 and 1982, and again from 1987 through 1996. This makes the goal hardly attainable. As a result of energetic promotion of the family planning policy through the campaign, the growth rate still dropped by 1.46% in a short period of time. In this sense, the campaign is effective and successful. By looking at figures indicating the percentage of people who have signed one-child pledges in both urban and rural areas, a fair judgment about the effectiveness of the campaign can be made.

In Beijing (an urban area) this percentage increased from 69.94% in 1979 to 98.41% in 1982. In rural areas, it increased from 22.44% in 1979 to 74.18% in 1982. In 1983, 70% to 90% of child bearing couples with one child in Sichuan, Jiangsu, Shanghai, Shandong and other major cities accepted the one-child certificates ("Population Control Is . . .," 1987). Although the figures vary from one place to another, the trend is that more and more people are practicing birth control.

The one-child family campaign is effective in terms of advocating the policy and reducing the growth rate. However, it has also produced some side effects the government did not foresee. One of the most noticeable side effects is the "spoiled child." Children in one-child families are often treated like kings and queens, whose parents and grandparents spoil, with too much attention. Another side effect is murder or abandonment of girl infants (especially in the countryside) when boys are strongly preferred.

The government has taken measures to address these side effects. For example, educational programs have been set up to teach parents how to raise physically as well as psychologically healthy single children in the family, and to teach the children to be caring, loving, and independent. Regarding the mistreatment of females, the government has established laws to protect women and girl infants. Similarly, it enforces severe punishment on those who mistreat women or girl infants.

We believe that the campaign has been successful in persuading people to practice family planning and in lowering population growth. Overall, Chinese society understands the necessity of the campaign. (I, the second author, initially viewed the one-child policy as barbaric until I visited China and saw what Chinese know all too well: there are too many people and not enough resources). As the government becomes more experienced in controlling population growth, it is hoped that the country will develop efficient methods for dealing with negative side effects of the campaign and that positive overall results will be realized. Analysis of the campaign, using Burke's rhetoric of transcendence, is intended to enhance understanding of campaign strengths and weaknesses.

References

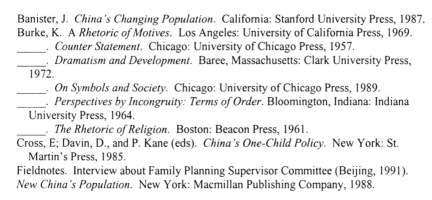

Banister, J. *China's Changing Population*. California: Stanford University Press, 1987.

Burke, K. A *Rhetoric of Motives*. Los Angeles: University of California Press, 1969.

_____. *Counter Statement*. Chicago: University of Chicago Press, 1957.

_____. *Dramatism and Development*. Baree, Massachusetts: Clark University Press, 1972.

_____. *On Symbols and Society*. Chicago: University of Chicago Press, 1989.

_____. *Perspectives by Incongruity: Terms of Order*. Bloomington, Indiana: Indiana University Press, 1964.

_____. *The Rhetoric of Religion*. Boston: Beacon Press, 1961.

Cross, E; Davin, D., and P. Kane (eds). *China's One-Child Policy*. New York: St. Martin's Press, 1985.

Fieldnotes. Interview about Family Planning Supervisor Committee (Beijing, 1991).

New China's Population. New York: Macmillan Publishing Company, 1988.

"Open Letter," *Report of the Central Committee of the Chinese Communist Party*. 1980.

"Population Control Is a Basic State Policy," *People's Daily* (September 16, 1987), p. 10.

"Population," *China: Facts and Figures*. Beijing: Foreign Language Press, 1984.

"Premier Zhao Ziyang Explains the Population Control Situation in China," *People's Daily* (September 19, 1987), p. 1.

Rogers, E.M. *Communication Strategies for Family Planning*. New York: The Free Press, 1973.

Stewart, C.J.; Smith, C.A.; and R.E. Denton. *Persuasion and Social Movements*. Proper Heights, New Jersey: Waveland Press Inc., 1984.

_____. *Persuasion and Social Movements (Second Edition)*. Prospect Heights, Illinois: Waveland Press, 1989.

"The Chinese Population Is Now Increasing in a Planned Manner," *People's Daily* (September 25, 1987), p. 4.

Zhao Ziyang. *Report of the Second Asian Population and Development Forum*. 1987.

Zhongshan University Journal. Zhongshan: Zhongshan University Press, 1984.

Conclusion

President Clinton's 1998 Trip to China:
High Context Diplomacy Balancing on Low Context Issues Expressed Through High Context Channels

In June and July 1998 President Bill Clinton visited China during a ten day period that included stops in Xi'an, Beijing, Guilin, Shanghai and Hong Kong. His trip included meetings with Chinese President Jiang Zemin and other Chinese leaders. Key issues intended for discussion during this trip included the opening of Chinese markets for U.S. trade, human rights abuses, the independence of Taiwan, and weapons proliferation. Clinton's trip, with a first stop in Xi'an and final stop in Hong Kong, received wide coverage in world media.

I was in China during the period leading up to Clinton's arrival, throughout his stay in China, and after his departure. I was in China in my capacity as Assistant Air Attaché to the U.S. Defense Attaché Office in Beijing. I am a Lieutenant Colonel in the Air Force reserve. I was in Beijing and then moved on to Xi'an to work Clinton's visit to Xi'an (his entry point into China). Four months later I served as the Defense Attaché Office Deputy Mission Commander for President Clinton's visit to Malaysia for the Asia-Pacific Economic Cooperation conference in Kuala Lumpur. This was my ninth visit to China and my fifth year serving as an Assistant Air Attaché to China. My previous assignment was with the Special Operations Command/Pacific at Camp Smith, Hawaii.

The issues addressed by Clinton during his visit were varied. Regarding the trade imbalance, there was a 49.7 billion dollar trade deficit between China and the U.S. during the 12 months leading up to the summit ("U.S. Warns of Sombre Impact...," *China News Digest*, 1998). The U.S. wants China to open its markets to more U.S. goods. Human rights was an issue in two main areas: the suppression of Tibet and religious and political freedom throughout China. The U.S. was also opposed to weapons sales by China to Pakistan and Iraq.

Probably the main long-standing issue dealt with the independence of Taiwan. Taiwan has functioned independently of China since the People's Republic of China was founded in 1949. Taiwan sees itself as a sovereign state, and China sees it as a renegade province that is part of China. China wants Taiwan to return fully to China, and the U.S. is adamant that Taiwan must have self-determination (which could include return to Chinese control, if Taiwan chooses). China is equally adamant that it is an internal matter in which the U.S. should not interfere.

These issues stressed at the summit had complexities inherent in the varied objectives of the parties concerned. However, it should be noted that these complexities were even more complex than an initial reading might convey, due to the differing cultural backgrounds in which they were rooted. China is a significantly different culture than the U.S., and the summit issues must be understood in light of this difference.

China has a huge population of 1.25 billion people, over four times that of the U.S., living in a land mass similar to the U.S. This is roughly one-fourth of the world's population. Most of these 1.25 billion people live in the eastern region of the country, particularly the eastern urban areas. In short, it is very crowded. The population size is an issue in and of itself (i.e., the one-child-per-family policy), and it is a factor that seeps into many other issues regarding life in China. The U.S. reader should consider how different life would be in his or her city or town if the number of inhabitants were multiplied by four-plus but the land mass remained the same. Friday afternoon rush hour would no doubt extend into Saturday morning.

China has been engaged in significant continual change for the past twenty years as it re-opens to the outside world. Although it has been a large-scale modernization process, Chinese culture has ancient roots, and the modernization rests on that foundation. In many respects its adoption of western technological innovations makes it seem similar to the U.S. but the context within which these changes occur is distinctly Chinese.

China's governance system is different than in the U.S. We usually think of this difference being expressed in terms of the Chinese maintaining socialism and communism and the U.S. maintaining capitalism and democracy. Equally important is that the Chinese do not stress rule of law as much as we do in the U.S. Decision making at all levels is very much affected by the political climate at that particular time.

This phenomenon is commensurate with the perspective conveying that China is a high context culture and the U.S. is a low context culture. That is, decision making (or having a sense of policy) in China requires a sense of context within which one exists, whereas in the U.S., which operates more in a low context system, one can seek explicitly stated laws, guidelines or policies that do not necessitate a grasp of prevailing political sensitivities. Awareness of such sensitivities can help promote a cause in the U.S., but, overall, the rule of law is primary.

Diplomacy tends to be a high context phenomenon. Often times symbolic means or gestures are used to express intention or point of view. This is done to avoid armed conflict, which is far more direct and representative of low context actions, and to avoid long term protracted disagreements. The U.S. practicing diplomacy in China has unique complexities because we are a low context culture practicing a high context phenomenon with (and in) a high context culture. This creates a situation where there is increased room for misunderstanding.

I will address some of the major issues of the summit, at one extreme, and some of the very minor issues I observed related to President Clinton's visit to Xi'an, at the other extreme. These representative issues are discussed because they exemplify high context diplomacy that occurred along with low context issues, both expressed through high context channels.

The biggest issue addressed during Clinton's visit dealt with the independence of Taiwan. Taiwan has been functioning independent of Chinese control since the founding of the People's Republic of China in 1949. China sees Taiwan as a renegade province and insists that Taiwan is an inalienable part of China. The U.S. affirms that Taiwan can return to Chinese control if it chooses but that Taiwan must exercise self-determination to do so and that there can be no use (or threat) of force by China to promote such a re-joining. While in Shanghai, Clinton seemed to back off of the U.S. position by stating that the U.S. is opposed to Taiwan independence and Taiwan joining the United Nations and other organizations in which membership would assume Taiwan independence ("Clinton: We Don't Support...," *China News Digest*, 1998). This statement gestured a softening of U.S. policy regarding the importance of Taiwan self-determination.

The U.S. Senate responded to Clinton's gesture with a rebuffing gesture of its own. "The U.S. Senate voted 92-0 to approve a resolution. . . that the future of Taiwan will be determined by peaceful means, with the consent of the people of Taiwan. . . (and) also reaffirmed Washington's commitment to help Taipei (the capital of Taiwan) maintain enough self-defense capability" ("U.S. Senate Passes Resolution. . .," *China News Digest*, 1998). The Chinese government "strongly condemned the U.S. Congress for its adoption of two resolutions that provide encouragement to the Taiwan administration. . . [and] reiterated Beijing's view that. . . the reunification of China is purely China's internal affair and no foreign interference will be allowed." ("Beijing Hits Out Against. . .," *China News Digest*, 1998).

Another high context issue that had political ramifications dealt with President Clinton being officially welcomed to Beijing in a Tiananman Square ceremony. In 1989, hundreds of participants in the (media dubbed) pro-demo-

cracy movement were gunned down by government troops in and around
Tiananman Square. For a U.S. president, leader of the free world, to participate
in such a ceremony at that location implied U.S. support for that Chinese
government action. Clinton was criticized for this, even before he left the U.S.,
by U.S. politicians and Chinese dissidents.

Clinton provided verbal (low context) clarification for any
misinterpretations of his appearance at Tiananman Square when, during a live
televised press conference with Chinese President Jiang Zemin, he stated, "I
believe, and the American people believe, that the use of force and the tragic
loss of life (in Tiananman Square) was wrong" ("T.V. Viewers Across. . .,"
China News Digest, 1998). Thus, on this issue, Clinton conveyed a high context
gesture to appease the Chinese government and followed it up with a low
context gesture to appease critics in the U.S. "Mr. Jiang,s words conveyed
important nuances to Chinese listeners. His characterization of Tiananman as a
'political disturbance' departed from the official line that it was a 'counter-
revolutionary riot'" ("Change in China," *International Herald Tribune*, 1998).

That the press conference occurred at all was equally important as the content
that was discussed. Such a press conference is common in the U.S. but unheard
of in China. "The two exchanged their opinions and answered reporters'
questions in front of a T.V. audience of millions of startled Chinese citizens who
heard for the first time a foreign leader speaking out about the Tiananman
Square crackdown. The nationally broadcast live press conference was
unprecedented, frank and open" ("T.V. Viewers Across...," *China News Digest*,
1998). The press conference, scheduled for 15 minutes, lasted 75 minutes.

Clinton scored points with U.S. religious leaders and human rights activists
by worshipping in a Beijing church as an expression of freedom of religion.
This action could also be construed as high context support for Tibetan
autonomy due to the unique religious foundation of Tibet. "Clinton told the
audience of about 2,300 that the Christian faith calls for unity of people around
the world. He also praised the growth of Christianity in China" ("Clinton
Attends Church . . .," *China News Digest*, 1998). The Chinese government is
usually strongly opposed to any organizations, especially those rooted outside of
China, that threaten control maintained by the Communist Party. The Chinese
saved face in this encounter because Clinton worshipped at Chungwenmen
Church, which is a government sanctioned church and, thus, an extension of the
government.

By the end of the summit, China and the U.S. had agreed on 47 issues that
were perceived to be mutually beneficial to both countries. These agreements
were in areas including economic and commercial, energy and
environment, enhancing arms control, human rights, law, military-to-military

relations, people-to-people exchanges, and political and security areas. An agreement, that was conveyed to the media as primary, was that the U.S. and China would de-target their nuclear warheads (that are aimed at each other), decreasing the possibility that there might be an accidental firing of deadly weapons. However, "it is widely acknowledged that a de-targeted nuclear device can be re-activated within a short span of time, perhaps only ten minutes" ("Presidents Jiang, Clinton Reach Agreements. . .," *China News Digest*, 1998). Regarding this agreement, a newspaper editorial stated, "They pretended that a symbolic agreement to re-target missiles had serious implications for stability" ("Candor in China," *International Herald Tribune*, 1998).

The issues described thus far deal with President Clinton's visit from a macro-level. These major issues addressed the primary reason for his visit to China. However, the role of high context communication channels illustrated in these primary issues is also illustrated in the micro-level issues that existed in relation to his trip. These minor issues and, in some cases, very minor issues consistently evidenced low context issues expressed through high context channels. I will draw from my experiences and observations in Xi'an, primarily at the airport, to illustrate this phenomenon. As noted earlier, I was in Xi'an as an Assistant Air Attaché from the Defense Attaché Office in Beijing.

I arrived in Xi'an six days before President Clinton arrived and stayed there 11 days. Relations with our Chinese counterparts were always cordial, but there was an underlying friction that existed regarding control. They perceived themselves to be in control insofar as it was their airport and city. We (U.S. representatives) perceived ourselves to be in control insofar as we had authority and responsibilities that were manifested in and conveyed through our standard operating procedures and objectives related to our support of a presidential visit. At times, notions of span of control overlapped with low context issues. These low context issues were typically expressed through high context channels. The following are representative examples.

The Air Force One (presidential plane) advance team, consisting of two officers, arrived in Xi'an and went through its checklist of requirements regarding Air Force One coming to Xi'an. The advance team members conveyed to the Chinese airport administration that when Air Force One landed at the airport they would handle all aspects of directing the aircraft to its resting place on the tarmac. No assistance from the Chinese was needed nor would any interference be permitted. It seemed like a relatively simple issue and there was no controversy related to this stipulation until minutes before Air Force One touched down at the Xi'an airport.

At that time, one of the Air Force One advance team officers was standing in place on the tarmac, batons in hand, to direct the Air Force One pilot to his parking place on the tarmac. The other officer was standing with the rest of us (U.S. and Chinese support organization members) and about 40 representatives from the international media. Members of the Secret Service, White House Communications, U.S. motorcade staff, and others were strategically placed to carry out their duties. The image conveyed in this scene clearly established that the U.S. support groups were in charge of the process.

Without warning, as cameras were clicking and video-cams recording, one of the Chinese engineers walked out on the tarmac with his batons in hand and stood next to the Air Force One advance team officer (who was directing Air Force One into place) as if he was co-directing the process. The Air Force One officer became emphatically insistent that the Chinese engineer vacate the tarmac because his being there ran the risk of confusing the Air Force One pilot. The Chinese engineer would not vacate the tarmac. Meanwhile, as somewhat of a side show, the media observed this issue of control. A quick compromise was achieved whereby the Chinese engineer could stand next to the Air Force One officer but not gesture in any way.

The U.S. personnel brought in to handle this operation were no doubt selected because of their high competency levels. I speculate that such high skill levels are frequently accompanied by a strong emphasis on stressing standards. It was my observation that cross-cultural understanding was secondary to mission objectives, as manifested in the behavior of both Americans and Chinese.

A few days before the President arrived, HMX-1 (the presidential helicopter) was flown in to Xi'an in a U.S. transport aircraft. There was much excitement when the U.S. C-5 (a very large aircraft) touched down at the Xi'an airport, given the friction that has occasionally existed between the U.S. and China over the years. A Chinese video cameraman taped the functioning of the aircraft. There were about 50 observers.

A security detail of U.S. Marines immediately surrounded the HMX-1 presidential helicopter when it was unloaded. They were clearly focused on their primary objective of protecting the helicopter, and they had no interest in entertaining Chinese inquisitiveness with the helicopter. The Chinese seemed mildly offended that they had to maintain a distance of at least six feet from the helicopter. The security guards clearly established their high context message of control over the situation.

However, within about 15 minutes, two Chinese workers came to the helicopter carrying a small spraying apparatus that resembled a fire extinguisher. Their stated directive, as immigration control officers, was to spray the tires of the helicopter with insecticide to ensure that no insect life was being imported on the helicopter. It hardly seemed necessary, but this was the objective.

It was drafty that day, and the HMX-1 pilot was fearful that the spray might mist onto the unique helicopter paint. It seemed to become a high context contest for control. There was mild shoving going on as the intended sprayer and his aide inched closer to the helicopter. A frustrated guard summoned my involvement with the predicament. I suggested a compromise whereby the insecticide could be applied to the helicopter tires with a paint brush but not with a sprayer. Both sides agreed.

Sometimes, issues would evolve without intention but intention would be perceived. This was a breeding ground for misunderstanding. Most of the U.S. military and Secret Service stayed in one hotel in Xi'an. I sensed a disgruntled attitude from some Marines one morning and quietly pursued the source of the disgruntlement. I then observed what they observed.

A worker at the hotel had been instructed to raise the U.S. flag so that it flew on a flag pole adjacent to the Chinese flag (an appropriate symbolic gesture). As he walked through the lobby, out the door, over the roadway and over to the flag poles, he loosely carried the U.S. flag in his left hand and it drug along the ground. Before he raised the Chinese flag, he dropped the U.S. flag on the ground so that he could use both hands to raise the Chinese flag. He then raised the U.S. flag.

Hoping to correct the situation, I approached the worker to advise him on our customs and courtesies regarding the handling of the U.S. flag. He conveyed, in my estimation, a lack of interest with my input, and I felt I could best modify the situation by seeking an intermediary. I had a vague suspicion that the Chinese flag was not treated as we treat the U.S. flag. I spoke to our hotel host, who helped us with a variety of logistical issues during our stay, and she advised the staff about our sensitivities. Our customs and courtesies with the U.S. flag were honored in coming days, but it took a while for the bad feelings to dissipate.

Another high context issue of control that occurred dealt with the periodic landings of our C-5 transport aircraft. The Chinese airport officials were mildly persistent about boarding each landing aircraft, as if they were officially sanctioned to inspect it. Our aircrew liaison staff rejected this insistence. Again, it seemed like a high context issue of clarifying who was in control between the owners of the aircraft and the keepers of the tarmac.

The Chinese gave in on this issue but gestured their overall control by slowing down their processing of the C-5 flight plans, in their Dispatch Office, because of (what seemed to me) fictitious policy infractions by the U.S. aircrews. Over time, as relations warmed among workers on the tarmac, the Chinese were invited onto some of the aircraft for tours as a goodwill gesture, the point being that they could board the aircraft, if invited, but they could not force their way on board. Again, this seemed a high context issue of control.

I had firsthand experience with the processing of U.S. aircraft flight plans. I picked up the flight plans from the pilots upon landing, took the flight plans to the Dispatch Office for processing and filing, and returned a copy of the flight plans to the aircraft. It is a fairly simple process that should not take more than 20 minutes in the Dispatch Office.

The first time I processed such a flight plan I encountered what I perceived to be a high context gesture from Dispatch Office personnel that they clearly had the upper hand in our relationship. The flight plan was rejected three times for menial reasons (flight altitude had been listed in feet instead of meters, some letters were not indicated in capital letters, and they did not want any pencil erasures or corrections on the form). It took 2 1/2 hours to process the flight plan.

The second time I brought in a flight plan, I did not even go to the counter to submit the plan. I sat in a chair patiently until someone inquired, after about 15 minutes, what I wanted. I submitted the form, and the plan was approved within 15 minutes. The third time I came in, I had the flight plan approved within 20 minutes and was offered tea while I waited. I cannot say for sure but I felt that a docile approach, signaling a high context acknowledgment that they were in control, helped me achieve objectives.

Tolerance for saving face, as a high context gesture, was important. One low context issue, an apparent theft, had to be handled via high context channels to achieve resolution. The U.S. rented locked warehouse space to secure equipment during our stay in Xi'an. One morning crew members noticed that 12 wooden pallets, that had been in the locked warehouse the night before, were missing. We reported the missing pallets to our Chinese counterparts and were flatly told that they were not stolen and that perhaps we misplaced them. This was very unlikely given the size of the pallets, that we were working in a very limited area and that crew members had just seen them the night before.

It became clear to us that, if we reported them as stolen, we probably would not be compensated for them. However, when we agreed that they were merely missing, we received a generous compensation subtracted from the expenditure total we owed them. Thus, tolerance for saving face helped us achieve our objectives.

In a more general sense, the role of context was very relevant in our day to day operations. Context provided the backdrop within which we functioned, much like weather does for a picnic. This was most noticeable when President Clinton arrived in Xi'an. The airport environment we worked in specifically, and the city of Xi'an in general, seemed to be filled with goodwill bordering on the euphoric. Somewhat adversarial relationships melted into quasi-friendships as we scrambled to get pictures with each other in front of Air Force One. We laughed and shared the excitement of the moment. It seemed like Christmas.

However, the context changed and the euphoria dissipated when Air Force One left Xi'an and moved on to Beijing. The party was over, and it was time to cleanup. The context changed.

This experience underscored the high context nature of diplomacy. Most of the issues had low context ramifications but these issues tended to be expressed through high context channels. This awareness helps one to better understand such events and enhances one's ability to function in such a setting. The Clinton trip to China offers insights regarding international diplomacy. Analysis of such phenomena, over time, offers conceptual frameworks that help us better understand the more closely linked world within which we live. This analysis is intended as a contribution to that understanding.

References

"Beijing Hits Out against Two Resolutions Passed by U.S. Senate," *China News Digest*, July 14, 1998.

"Candor in China," *International Herald Tribune*, July 4, 1998, p. 8.

"Change in China," *International Herald Tribune*, July 3, 1998, p. 10.

"Clinton Attends Church Services in Beijing," *China News Digest*, June 28, 1998.

"Clinton: We Don't Support Independence for Taiwan," *China News Digest*, July 2, 1998.

"Presidents Jiang, Clinton Reach Agreements in Historic Summit," *China News Digest*, June 27, 1998.

"T.V. Viewers Across Mainland Treated to Presidential Debate," *China News Digest*, June 28, 1998.

"U.S. Senate Passes Resolution to Reiterate Taiwan Policy," *China News Digest*, July 10, 1998.

"U.S. Warns of Sombre Impact of Trade Deficit on June Summit," *China News Digest*, April 16, 1998.

Index

About the Author

Jim Schnell is a Professor of Communication Studies at Ohio Dominican College in Columbus, Ohio. He completed his Ph.D. at Ohio University in 1982 and has authored three books, more than 40 journal articles, and more than 100 conference presentations dealing with interpersonal and cross-cultural communication. He has been to China nine times and taught as a visiting professor at Northern Jiaotong University (Beijing, China). Schnell is a Lieutenant Colonel in the U.S. Air Force (Reserve), where he is an Assistant Air Attaché to China.